D1529038

The
No-Øs Of
Leadership

Aspirations on being
a Leader Worth Following
from a 20-year journey
as a CEO

ISBN: 9798408015535

Imprint: Independently published

This book was produced in collaboration with Write Business
Results Limited. For more information on their business book, blog
and podcast services, please visit www.writebusinessresults.com
or contact the team via info@writebusinessresults.com.

 WRITE BUSINESS RESULTS

The
No-Øs Of
Leadership

Aspirations on being a Leader Worth Following from a 20-year journey as a CEO

SELF-AWARENESS

EMPATHY

EGO

LIBIDO

DINERO

MIKE EASLEY

"Mike Easley was an active and excited learner in the executive development program at Grand Canyon University and I admire his constant desire to be a better leader. Whether you are an individual just learning about self-leadership, a more experienced manager working on developing your skills as a team leader, or a seasoned servant leader at the executive level, *The No-Os of Leadership* is well worth the read. Mike's words are meaty and motivating as he speaks directly to you with leadership lessons from his own life and work – from Scout to CEO – that are real and relatable. This enjoyable book will leave you wanting more from Mike." – *Ken Blanchard, Co-Author of The One Minute Manager® and Simple Truths of Leadership*

"Mike has undertaken the difficult task of providing a practical guide to leadership skills. Skills essential in our work and home life. Rarely do leadership books admit mistakes made by the author. Mike's skills developed in the 'school of hard knocks' which is simply code for learning from our mistakes and our successes. Read the book and you will make fewer mistakes and claim greater success." – *Governor Dave Freudenthal, Former Governor, State of Wyoming*

"If you didn't have a title would anyone follow you? The underlying message of this delightful book is that leadership is a choice. In fact, it's hundreds of choices, every day, that revolve around knowing yourself, growing yourself and then lifting others to do something far more spectacular together than you ever could on your own. Advocating for the kind of leadership our world needs right now, Easley nails it! Apply these principles and become a leader people love to follow." – *Kevin Freiberg, Ph.D.*

"Mike is a legend across the Rockies for his leadership, his public service and his humility. He is literally the last person in the region to promote himself. This enduring reputation makes his advice valuable, both as food for thought and as a model to emulate." – *Ted Ladd, Dean and Professor at Hult, Instructor at Harvard and Wyoming entrepreneur*

"Mike Easley deftly distills 25 years of CEO experience into a clear, practical and effective guide for how to avoid the common pitfalls, mistakes and traps awaiting anyone undertaking a journey into leadership. What's more, readers will emerge enriched and prepared from his counsel on how to become the best version of themselves as a leader – the version worth following!" – *Tim Sullivan, President and CEO, Wright-Hennepin Cooperative Electric Association*

"Simply reading this book, I think I became a better person by osmosis! I appreciate Mike's insights, actionable tips on leadership, and writing style. But the real reason I urge you to read this book is because of his humanity, empathy, and heartfelt good intentions. To paraphrase one of my favorite movie lines (Jack Nicholson tells his girlfriend, played by Helen Hunt in the movie *As Good As It Gets*, "You make me want to be a better man."): Mike makes me want to be a better leader." – *Susan Fowler, Author of Master Your Motivation*

"Effective leadership requires relentless honesty, focus and effort. Mike's keen ability to use his own experiences to distill proven leadership techniques paves the way for a new generation of electric co-op leaders." – *Jim Matheson, Chief Executive Officer, National Rural Electric Cooperative Association*

CONTENTS

ACKNOWLEDGEMENTS

I would not be where I am today were it not for Ken Blanchard and the Ken Blanchard Executive MBA at Grand Canyon University. To spend a year in dialogue with Ken Blanchard and his team, exploring the essence of leadership, is something I will never forget and is something that has helped and driven me to aspire to be a Leader Worth Following. Were it not for my friend Kevin Freiberg, I would have never had the courage and GUTS to take on such a huge challenge nor, at the sunset of my career as an electric cooperative CEO, to put pen to paper to share the story in hopes that others may also embark on their journey to be a Leader Worth Following.

DEDICATION

I have had an amazing career in the electric cooperative industry. It has spanned nearly four decades working alongside so many good people, numerous teams and four electric cooperatives in Oklahoma, Alaska, Michigan and Wyoming. I dedicate this book to my electric cooperative family. You have all helped me grow out of engineering and grow into leadership. That growth was painful for me, and maybe for you too. I am sure my wake was difficult to manage through in the earlier years and I hope it became easier as I grew as a leader.

My hope for each of you is to be the best possible version of yourself and to be a Leader Worth Following. Perhaps this book may provide you a few takeaways to help you on that journey. I have tried to pass on some lessons I have learned along the way, in hopes that your leadership journey and growth as a person can take you beyond your wildest dreams and expectations, as my lessons and experiences did for me. Perhaps this book will help you have a smoother and easier journey than mine.

Being a Leader Worth Following is a noble calling and if this book helps you reach that goal, even in some small way, my journey will have been that much richer and fulfilling.

FOREWORD

Leaders are learners who teach. What you hold in your hands are the practical, yet hard-won insights from a seasoned executive who would like nothing more than to cut your cycle time on becoming a leader people love to follow and on moving yourself, your team and your organization to the next level of good.

Mike Easley doesn't write from a position of having arrived. In fact, he would tell you that he is still very much in process – a leadership journey for which there is no destination.

That said, the lessons you are about to learn come from one who has been in the trenches of leadership for over two decades. As the saying goes, "No pressure, no diamond." Mike has felt the pressure of leading a board of directors in a time of crisis, rallying a team facing seemingly insurmountable challenges, changing a tired culture, and figuring out how to serve a community facing significant environmental, technological, political, and social disruption.

Easley has done this in one of the noblest movements in our country: the cooperative movement. Cooperatives are unique in that they were built by the people, for the people. Many are volunteers elected to positions by peers in their communities. From stay-at-home parents to seasoned executives, they bring a wide array of experience, or inexperience, to the game. These people do not see their organizations as grocery chains, banks, and utilities; they see them as member-centric movements fighting for the "little" person. It takes a special kind of leadership to play and succeed in this arena. Mike Easley has done both.

Frankly, the insights contained here are not new. Unlike so many leadership books that try to be cute by dressing up the same doll with different clothes (by which I mean adjectives), Mike takes a straightforward approach to opening the kimono and letting you in on his leadership journey. The takeaways in this book have been tested and they work. I respect that.

Name your arena: business, politics, community, or marriage and family – almost every failure in leadership can be traced back to a failure of nerve. This book calls out that problem and invites you to be courageous.

WARNING! While the ideas here may not be new, putting them into practice is not for the faint of heart. Execution is hard. Easley invites you to discover your blind spots and become self-aware. Of course, this means you have to be vulnerable, courageous and smart enough to ask for help. The higher you go in an organization the harder this is because people are less willing to give you feedback. This is why leaders engage trusted advisors like Mike Easley. It's lonely at the top and executives need someone they can talk to, someone they can trust, who will talk straight.

Many years ago, my wife and business partner, Jackie and I met Jimmy Blanchard, former CEO of one of the largest credit card processing companies in the world, Synovus Financial. Jimmy was famous for holding all-employee meetings and asking, "What are the 10 dumbest things we do around here, starting with me?" Jimmy was one of those rare CEOs who wanted to become more self-aware and learn how he landed on people.

As Easley so aptly states, "You can't fix a problem if you don't know it exists." Jimmy Blanchard was willing to face the brutal facts of reality, identify the fault lines in his organization, and dig deep to make the necessary changes.

Thanks to the internet, we live in a world of transparency where incidents and behaviors go viral in a heartbeat. It is also a world where people are so easily offended. This causes many leaders to armor up, pose, and pretend for fear that someone – customer/client, board member, regulator, reporter, or employee, just to name a few – will call them out. The problem is that people see right through the facade, and then the leader loses credibility and becomes someone people don't want to follow.

This book calls us all to a higher level of leadership – a leadership that challenges us to give presence to our teammates, to never walk past a problem, to choose service over self-interest, to admit when we are wrong; and to then engage in the art of the apology and find the courage to change. We are invited to trade ego, power and money for fighting a cause that enriches lives and makes the world, at least our little corner of it, better.

But in *The No-Os of Leadership,* Mike Easley doesn't leave us there. He gives us the strategies and tools to do it based on what's worked and what hasn't in his own experience as a CEO... as a human being.

As a thought leader and practitioner who cares deeply about enriching the lives of others, he is committed to a never-ending search for finding better, more efficient ways to inspire people to change.

Kevin Freiberg

Ph.D. Co-author of the bestselling books: *NUTS! Southwest Airlines' Crazy Recipe for Business and Personal Success; CAUSE! A Business Strategy for Standing Out in a Sea of Sameness;* and *Bochy Ball! The Chemistry of Winning and Losing in Baseball, Business and Life.*

Sundance, UT, November 2021

PREFACE

One of the most important elements of leadership is knowing your story as a leader, what shaped you, where you come from, and then communicating that to your team. It's also important to make a practice of reviewing and keeping in touch with your story. One of the best ways I've found to do this is to create a Leadership Point of View.

I wish I could say that I invented the Leadership Point of View, but I first learned about this approach from Ken Blanchard when I was studying under him for my Ken Blanchard MBA at Grand Canyon University. Through this process, you explore the leadership influences over your life and really hone in on your values, your expectations of self and others, and who you are as a leader.

I have delivered my Leadership Point of View to my team and incorporated this process into our leadership development program at Powder River Energy, so all our aspiring leaders can create their own Leadership Point of View document. I'm presenting my Leadership Point of View as the preface to this book to honor that practice and to give you an example of what a Leadership Point of View looks like in hopes that you will start yours. The Leadership Point of View is the first step in becoming a Leader Worth Following. After 20 years, I still hope to be that kind of leader and I hope, in some small way, that you too may aspire to this journey as you write your own leadership story.

I also hope sharing my Leadership Point of View will help you start to think about how developing your own Leadership Point of View could enhance your leadership abilities and your relationships with your team. More importantly, I wanted to share it to plant the seed that if you find yourself in a position to mentor and lead, or to be part of developing a team or an individual's leadership skills, that you may consider passing on the torch that I picked up from Ken Blanchard and help others aspire to be a Leader Worth Following.

My Leadership Point of View

My Mentors...

I have been blessed with many mentors in my life; each of them appearing at the right time and place.

When I think about the most influential people in my life, the first person that comes to mind is my maternal grandfather. My Grandpa's greatest gift to me was teaching me about work ethic. To my Grandpa, the measure of a man was how hard he worked. In my Grandpa's opinion, it did not matter if you wore gloves to work or wore a tie. What mattered was that you gave it your all, for as long as it took to get the job done.

He encouraged me to go to college by telling me that he never had the opportunity to attend past an eighth-grade education. At the same time, he would tell me that 50 cents and my college diploma would get me a cup of coffee. My most memorable experience of my Grandpa's leadership style happened on my 13th birthday. My Grandpa came into my room at 7 a.m., woke me up and quickly put me to work in the yard filling in ditches. I was crushed that I had to work on my birthday. My Grandpa told me that I was a man now and would be working on my birthday for the rest of my life.

Finally, when the day was done at about 4 p.m., my Grandpa gave me $10. I was totally shocked since my wage working with him during the summer was $1 per day. He must have seen the look on my face because he looked me straight in the eye and said, "Work like a man, get paid like a man." My Grandpa was never one for many words.

Jack Hwang is the Grand Master of a Tae Kwon Do school. Mr. Hwang is a very humble and quiet man. I learned the Tae Kwon Do "Aims to Achieve" during the years I was an active student, and internalized them during the years that I taught Tae Kwon Do. Integrity, perseverance, indomitable spirit, courtesy, and self control are the "Aims to Achieve", or Tenets, of Tae Kwon Do. It wasn't until I tested for my 4th degree black belt that I finally understood that Mr. Hwang's style of leadership required that in order to achieve mastery, you must humble yourself and serve your students.

The literal translation for Tae Kwon Do is "Hand and Foot Way", but the true meaning of "Way" is the true pearl of wisdom that was passed to me by Mr. Hwang. Most people would assume the meaning of "Way" was direction, manner, or method. While this is partially correct, the true meaning of "Way" is what happens when a doctor helps a patient, a teacher teaches a student, or a parent helps a child with a bruised knee. "Way" is about the basic "helping and healing" of people. In that context, Tae Kwon Do is not about learning how to use your hands and feet in self-defense, but it is about using your hands and feet in helping, healing, and teaching.

In my professional experience, I have been blessed with wonderful mentors and many of them actually knew that they were mentors to me. Clearly, the most influential person in this area was Doug Bursey. Doug is a huge man, both in stature and presence. Most people I knew absolutely hated working for him. Doug had a very odd and unnerving way of staring at a person. His gaze would penetrate your soul and any uncertainty you had would reverberate with fear under his scrutiny.

Doug had a way of asking more of you than you thought you were capable of doing. He would throw you in the deep end, and would not come in after you until he sensed you were going down for the third time. When I worked for Doug, I did the impossible and I stretched beyond anything I thought I could do. I was one of the few privileged people who Doug let see past his crusty, rugged exterior. I saw this side of Doug one evening when we met the bereaved wife of a lineman who had just been fatally burned in an electrical contact accident on the job. From Doug, I learned that you could be tough on the outside and tender on the inside.

The strongest mentor in my life has been my maternal grandmother, or Grandma. She is a powerful prayer warrior and has held me accountable to myself and to God. She told me on her 80th birthday that she is finally beginning to see things as they are, and that she was so foolish in her 60s.

My Purpose...

At the core of my being is the need to fix things.

The bigger the mess, the more I like it! I also like to solve problems by simply looking at them from a different perspective. Oftentimes, if you are able to convey this perspective to others, you experience that "Ah Ha" moment. This has occurred numerous times in my business career where I challenged the assumed constraints and did things that could not be done according to conventional wisdom. The saying that you should call an expert if you want to find out how not to do something rings true with me. I want to quietly go about making things better. I am inspired to make a positive difference and to leave things better than when I found them.

My Values...

Integrity, Perseverance, Courtesy, Self-Control, and Indomitable Spirit are my core values.

I know I am living these values when I look at myself in the mirror and feel no twinge of regret or wave of remorse in what I have said, done, or thought.

My father's greatest gift to me was his living example of "taking personal responsibility". My father has struggled since his return from Vietnam and did not find himself until he graduated from college when I was in the ninth grade. Through all the moves from one job to another while I was growing up, my dad never let his family know of his inner demons. Personal responsibility lies at the foundation of my core values; for without this foundation there would be no driving force to maintain these values.

I am firmly convinced that there are three No-Os of leadership that create fatal flaws in leadership. These are ego, libido and dinero. If you can be aware of these No-Os and take personal responsibility for how you lead, you can avoid the carnage of leadership failures involving any one, or a combination of, the No-Os.

My Leadership Vision...

I truly want to be a Leader Worth Following.

I have sought leadership positions since I was very young. At first I liked leadership because of the freedom and the choices due to the sense of being in charge that came with it. Through my young adulthood I felt as though I deserved to be the leader since I felt competency and commitment to the task at hand were the prerequisites for leadership.

Now in midlife, and definitely past "mid-career", I see leadership as a heavy load that, under the right conditions, can be easily borne; and under the wrong circumstances is a crushing burden. I have seen the impact of my decisions played out in the reality of people's lives, and because of that I am increasingly motivated and inspired to be the best leader I can be – not so much for me, but for the people whose lives I impact as I lead.

My Promise...

If people will let me lead them, they can expect that I will give 110% and I will not quit on them.

I will hold true to my core values and my faith in both my professional and personal life. I will try to learn something new every day. I will not ask them to do anything that I would not be willing to do myself. I will open myself to their feedback and be willing to hear all things. I will not take their harsh criticism personally; however, I will not be immune to the pain of hurt feelings.

I will be compassionate as I point out areas for improvement in others and be grateful for having things pointed out to me that I could improve. I will do my best to help them meet challenges.

My Expectations...

I expect my people to be hard-working, honest, value-centered, and to avoid the No-Os of Leadership.

I realize that some people can work "harder" than others and, on any given day, one's ability to work hard varies. My expectations for them to be honest, value-centered and to avoid the No-Os of leadership do not vary from person to person, or from situation to situation. I expect people to be honest with themselves as well as with the people around them. I expect people to have compassion for each other and, while it's not so much an expectation, I would very much appreciate them having compassion for me.

My Example...

Next to me giving my word, giving my example is the most powerful way I can show my commitment to be a Leader Worth Following.

I demonstrate my desire to learn and to grow by looking for ways to learn new things and to revitalize things that I might have overlooked or underused. I keep myself mentally sharp and physically strong by taking care of myself and making positive choices in what I do to and with my body. I learn from my mistakes by admitting them and making a sincere effort to do better next time. I strive to demonstrate integrity in my relationships, my actions, and my decisions.

I invite you to join me as we explore lessons in leadership that have been learned over my life's experience and by attending the "school of hard knocks". We can make the world a better place by doing our part to make ourselves better leaders. If you have just one take away from this book, you can make a difference as you aspire to be a Leader Worth Following.

INTRODUCTION

I consider myself to be a student of leadership. Although I've been the CEO at Powder River Energy Corporation (PRECorp) for over 20 years, I know there are always new things for me to learn as a leader. During my time in the Ken Blanchard EMBA program at Grand Canyon University, Ken Blanchard taught me that there is a continuum of leadership, which begins with self-leadership and progresses through team leadership and then to organizational leadership.

This book is designed to support you as you move along that journey. Whether you are aspiring to become a leader, or are in a leadership position and just want to improve your leadership skills, I hope you will find useful insights and information in the following pages.

Over the years I've developed a tool called the No-Os of Leadership, which is a useful tool in your own self-awareness as a leader. These No-Os are what I describe as leadership landmines that can take you down as a leader. They are ego, libido and dinero. The antidotes to these No-Os are self-awareness and empathy.

As we've continued our leadership development program at PRECorp, and as I've mentored leaders, I highlight these No-Os to help them maintain awareness of these potential traps. I also encourage my team and those I mentor to bring in the No-Os construct when they are making decisions and to even identify leadership failures they see around them in the context of the No-Os. They might even recognize one of the No-Os in a leadership failure of their own.

Throughout this book, I'll share leadership stories and relate those to the No-Os and their antidotes – self-awareness and empathy – to help you to start looking at both leadership challenges and successes through that lens.

I've written this book in three parts, each one discussing a different stage on that leadership continuum. In Part 1, we begin by exploring the idea of self-leadership. The qualities I highlight here are the necessary foundations for developing as a good leader. The concept of self-awareness starts here, but it's a common thread that weaves throughout a leadership journey and one that is present at every point on the leadership continuum.

In Part 2, we discover how to move into effectively leading teams. If you have mastered self-leadership, this step will feel natural. This section of the book covers building and developing teams, and individuals within your teams, while also developing your own experience and abilities as a leader.

Finally, in Part 3, we look at organizational leadership and how your approach to leadership needs to change as you shift to this final stage of the continuum where you're leading multiple teams rather than a single team. This is where I'll explore the No-Os of Leadership in greater detail, which are those three areas of ego, libido and dinero that I believe leaders need to be particularly aware of and avoid if they are to make decisions that truly serve their organization, the people around them, and the greater good. I also look at the magic that happens in the boardroom and the importance of the board-CEO relationship, particularly in electric cooperatives.

Throughout this book, I've shared my own leadership stories and the learnings I have taken from experiences throughout my career. I hope that these help to put some of the concepts I talk about into context and give you a clearer understanding of how they can manifest along your own leadership journey.

One overriding theme is that good leadership is about finding ways to serve your people. These people include not only your employees, but also your customers and external stakeholders. The benefit of having this focus at an organizational level is significant. It leads to greater business success, it leads to a company culture with engaged and thriving employees, and it will allow you to develop new leadership talent that is ready for the challenges every business faces in an increasingly uncertain world.

The concept of service is especially imperative in electric cooperatives. These are not-for-profit electric utilities that span the majority of the geographical footprint of the US and that have been in existence since 1935. When they were first established they were a huge part of providing a higher quality of life to people across the US, and especially in rural America. Because cooperatives are not-for-profit, they focus on service to their members (customers) as opposed to being served by them.

In order to have a genuine focus on service, the leaders of these organizations and their employees must be thinking about serving, rather than being served. This means the levers that we have to pull as leaders in a not-for-profit entity that is focused on service will be much more different than the levers leaders have to pull in a for-profit company that is focused primarily on the bottom line. My hope is that some of the aspects of my leadership journey presented in this book will help you discover the reasons why you want to lead, how you can be a better leader to your people and, ultimately, how you can serve your own members in the best way possible.

"Think about your own life and be honest with yourself. Don't you ultimately get your greatest joy, find your deepest meaning and feel the most 'on purpose' when you are serving – serving your spouse, your kids, your organization and/or your community?"

These days, people are looking for jobs that have meaning, rather than just jobs that make them a living. The approach to leadership and the leadership model that I'll share with you in the following chapters supports the creation of meaning within an organization; and that in turn provides meaning to every individual working within that organization.

This could not be more timely as we all come out of the first two years of the Covid-19 pandemic. The pace of change and the need for great leadership was accelerated during this time. People and organizations are now playing a game of 52-Card Pickup. This game is played by taking a nicely ordered deck of cards and throwing them up in the air. The Covid-19 pandemic took our neatly stacked deck of priorities and tossed them in the air. As people and organizations began picking up those cards, we were tossing out ones we don't need and reordering those we do. The best leaders will be cognizant of this and do it with intention and compassion for themselves, their teams, and their organization.

As you move along your leadership journey, I want you to know that you're not alone in facing challenges and issues. Know that there are always solutions to problems you may be facing, even if you're not able to see them just yet. In taking the time and effort to develop yourself as a leader, you're coming one step closer to finding them. Facing issues and challenges can be really scary, but if you can reframe your thinking to see them as learning opportunities, you will have taken a big step forward in your growth journey.

PART 1:

Self-Management/ Self-Focus

Your journey as a leader starts by leading yourself. The concepts of self-management and self-focus are important to create the awareness needed for being a leader. Your personal growth journey may not be one that is focused on being formally recognized as a leader, but everyone can benefit from growth opportunities around self-leadership.

Even as a young child, there are opportunities for leadership. Maybe you were the kid who organized games, or maybe you were the kid who laid out the rules. Even in play, these are real steps along the journey of leadership.

As you get older, things begin to get a little more formal. You'll have different opportunities, whether through school or extracurricular activities. When you look at the people who naturally take to being leaders early on, you can identify some common characteristics among them. These people usually have lots of focus, they're able to self-regulate, they have self-discipline and they know what they want. True leaders genuinely care about other people and truly want to help them.

Although you could argue that most people know what they want, the people who develop most quickly as leaders not only know what they want, but they also have the focus and desire to go after it and do what they need to do to work towards it. This is where the qualities of self-management and self-focus come into play.

When we go into the workplace, most of us don't start at the top. We have to work our way up through the ranks, learning our job or profession as we go. However, it's these qualities of self-management and self-focus that really help you to stand out and be recognized by the leaders in any organization; and it's your ability to work well with others and support and serve your team that lays the foundation for your leadership journey.

Good leaders are constantly looking at their people to find the ones who have the most potential, and then coaching them along their leadership journey.

Being able to focus on yourself and understand your motivation is what helps to get you recognized and it's your desire to serve others that will set you apart. This sets off a virtuous cycle where the characteristics of focus, self-discipline, dependability, and service ensure you're recognized. You are then fed work and opportunities to continue your development of those skills and become better at what you do.

"The greatest character strength and the greatest virtue is **Love**. *And what does love look like? It looks like* **Service**.*"*

I believe all leaders need to be highly self-aware. The very first step on any leadership journey starts with managing yourself and displaying those qualities of focus, self-discipline, dependability and, most importantly, service.

If you're a first-time leader, or an aspiring leader, the first thing you have to do to move along your leadership journey and start having increased responsibilities is to show that you're effective at leading yourself. Being aware of this need to have motivation, being self-disciplined and dependable, and working on developing these qualities, is very important if you want to aspire to greater leadership positions.

If you already hold a leadership position, it's good to reflect on where you've been on your journey. Even if you're only leading a few people, it's very important to reflect on how you got to where you are, especially if you want to continue to grow as a leader, and take on higher levels of responsibility and service to your teams.

In my opinion, one of a leader's jobs is to develop their team and give their people opportunities to continue to grow. If you have folks on your team who you feel have leadership potential, helping them understand how their self-leadership will prepare them for their own journey is an important part of your role. This also feeds into your own development as a leader. Your ability to tell stories and describe some of the things that have helped you develop as a leader are also really important if you're aspiring to greater levels of responsibility and leadership.

This is why we'll begin in Chapter 1 by exploring what I believe are four of the most important characteristics to develop for self-management and self-awareness: motivation, self-discipline, dependability and service to others.

CHAPTER 1: MOTIVATION

"The positive effects of optimal motivation will give you energy and the ability to keep going when others might give up."

Motivation is why people do what they do. We all have motivation. Understanding what your motivators are can help you get things done and accomplish the goals you've set for yourself.

When we're thinking about motivators in terms of ourselves, it quickly becomes clear that understanding our motivators helps us to accomplish our goals and even has an effect on the internal conversations we have with ourselves. Susan Fowler, author of *Master Your Motivation*[1], discusses the new science of optimal motivation and identifies three things that produce it. These are choice, connection, and competence. Creating choice, connection, and competence will serve you well in your leadership journey. When it comes to starting your leadership journey, I think there are three elements that will help you stay on track. They are: focus, self-regulation and dependability.

Focusing on what you want, in spite of distractions, is necessary in order to accomplish anything. Self-regulation is about remembering what it is you want to achieve and being able to intentionally avoid the things that take you off track in the pursuit of that goal. Dependability is about being consistent and knowing that you can rely on yourself and that others can rely on you.

---

1 Susan Fowler, (2019), *Master Your Motivation: Three Scientific Truths*, Berrett-Koehler Publishers

Others also need to see these three qualities in you. They need to know they can rely on you to stay on course through your self-discipline and that you have enough focus to keep your eye on the target and avoid getting distracted along the way. This is why I believe these three elements are so important for leaders to understand and develop within themselves right from the beginning of their leadership journey.

Building blocks for leadership

Focus, self-regulation, dependability, and service are characteristics that people will recognize in you quite early on in your leadership journey. Anyone who has these qualities – whether in the workplace or elsewhere, whether young or old – will be easy to lead. This is what will also get you noticed as a potential future leader.

If you're leading a team, and there's one person who has more focus, more self-regulation and is more dependable than someone else, you will rely on them to help get things done. This, in turn, sets the stage for them to become a leader, whether formally or informally, in the future.

The concepts of focus, self-regulation, dependability and service don't really change, regardless of the stage in your leadership journey. What may change, however, are the things underneath those characteristics. What creates that focus might be different in your 20s than it is in your 40s, for instance.

Dependability might look different early in your career than it does later on. Early on, it may be as simple as showing up when you've committed to do so. As you grow in your work and position, the idea of dependability is still there, but it might look different compared to those early stages of your career.

While the way these qualities are displayed might change, what I believe doesn't change is the necessity of having these qualities in the first place. If you don't have focus, self-regulation, dependability and service, you won't really get out of the blocks to begin your leadership journey. Let's unpack each of these qualities a little further.

Focus

Focus varies from person to person, but the way I describe it is as a sense of positive urgency that builds inside a person to help them move towards an end goal. This sense of positive urgency can be fed in different ways, depending on what's going on in your life. If your sense of urgency is fear-based, your motivation will be suboptimal. If your urgency comes from a need to please, you might be struggling with forming healthy connections. Perhaps your urgency is based on a lack of confidence, in which case you might have some challenges related to competency. The best motivation comes from positive urgency that links to your purpose and values, contributes to the welfare of others, and involves learning and growth for yourself and others. As humans, we tend to function along a continuum where we are in motion towards a goal, aspiration, or outcome. Perhaps your motivation is not optimal all the time, but you do the work to be self-aware and feed yourself healthy self-talk to develop a mindset that brings with it choices, connection, and competence.

For example, somebody may have a really high desire to please others and be recognized for a job well done. While they feel motivated to get things done, this type of suboptimal motivation may leave them feeling depleted. Instead consider shifting your thinking about the job by recognizing choices, how it helps people, and how you may grow from it. This type of motivation, optimal motivation, will give you energy and fill you up.

We all have responsibilities in our personal lives that we're trying to fulfill, whether that's providing for our families or providing for ourselves. That can help us stay focused as well. For other people, their focus can come from a belief around the way the world needs to look or behave in relation to a particular issue.

It's not only having this focus that tends to make people good leaders, but also being aware of that focus and what's behind it. One person may be inspired by multiple factors in their lives and it won't always be the same thing that they focus on every day. Someone who is aware of the importance of creating choice, connection and competency in themselves and others will create optimal motivation for themselves and others. The positive effects of optimal motivation will give you energy and the ability to keep going when others might give up.

Some days might be more difficult than others and you might need to draw on different aspects of those elements to compel you through the day, the week, or to get to the end of a project. Drawing from an aligned set of values, a noble purpose and the love of serving others will be helpful to get through these days. As you're trying to develop your leadership, it's essential to be aware of what is important to you so that you can tap into these optimal motivators to keep yourself moving, focused and filled with positive energy.

Being able to identify what is important to others is also helpful when you're leading them, because you will be looking for the next leaders you can develop. Understanding other people will help you, as the leader, do a better job of developing those future leaders and giving them opportunities. It is important that we balance what is important to us along with the needs of others and how we can all serve the common good.

Understand yourself first

Understanding yourself is the key to being able to motivate and manage yourself. Understanding the power of framing things through the lens of choice, connection, and competence can feed your motivators. You can use this mindset to help you show up to do the best you can do in being able to lead yourself – an essential step to take before you can lead others.

There are obviously different ways of managing and leading yourself as you follow your leadership journey, but you always have to be mindful about how this might impact others. Without self-awareness, focus may not always be helpful.

Imagine you're driving a speedboat racing across the water, and that you're the kind of person who leaves a pretty big wake behind you. As your boat goes by, it creates big waves that rock and crash into everything around them, knocking people over. If you're the kind of person who leaves a big wake behind them that disrupts other people, whether you're in a leadership position or just self-leading, it's a sign that you're not entirely aware of yourself and that your focus may not be healthy for either you or the people around you.

This links back to the concepts of self-awareness and self-focus. If you understand yourself and your motivation and you're aware of the impact of that on others around you, it helps you as a leader. This self-awareness also encompasses some of the other characteristics you need to develop for self-leadership that we'll talk about later in this first part. Responsibility, in particular, springs to mind in that it's your personal responsibility to make sure you don't leave a damaging wake as you move through life and work.

Self-regulation

In simple terms, focus is remembering why you're doing something and what you're trying to accomplish, as well as how you're going to achieve your goal. Self-regulation is discerning the thoughts and actions that keep you moving forward along your chosen path. Self-awareness can help you remember what you want, analyze what you are doing to get there and make the adjustments needed to keep yourself on track.

Your values are one element that underpins your self-regulation. As a leader, and especially an early leader or self-leader, it's important to understand the values and ethics that are guiding you as you move through life. The life lessons you've learned, your behaviors and ways of thinking about things, over time, translate into values.

One value that might guide you is being truthful, for example. I think we all learn at an early age that being truthful helps us accomplish our goals and get what we need in the long run. As we've gone through our lives, most of us have discovered that being truthful is the better path.

If we look at the idea of self-regulation in the context of the value of truth, we remember that being truthful is important. We know that it will help us accomplish our goal and we've learned that things work out better by being truthful. Therefore, when we're given the opportunity, we choose to be truthful. The self-regulation comes in when we choose this path even when it might be easier to hide, avoid or shade the truth. Remembering that being truthful is important to us and important for our outcomes is an act of self-awareness.

Of course there are many other values; truth is just one of them. The point is that, when you have self-regulation, you're able to take the things you've learned on your life's journey – either through experience or observation – and apply those consistently to your actions and choices.

Self-regulation involves identifying the behaviors that help us accomplish our goals and work well with others, and then applying them. Dependability, which I'll talk more about shortly, is another example that comes to mind.

We have to practice self-regulation in many areas of our lives, though. We are constantly bombarded by many things in our daily lives and we need to have the focus to not be distracted by all the other matters that may be pulling at us. It could be our phones, Facebook messages, or any other number of distractions. Being aware of those distractions and not allowing them to draw our focus takes self-regulation.

As a leader, if you look at somebody and can see they have focus, a purpose and are motivated to accomplish a goal or task – as well as having the self-regulation to remember both why that goal is important and what they need to do to accomplish that goal – you are likely to see them as dependable.

You can count on them to not only have the ability to accomplish goals, but also to be able to keep focused in a positive direction. As soon as they are doing this consistently, they become dependable. This makes it easy for people to give them greater responsibility.

If having increased responsibility and levels of leadership is important to you, you would do well to understand how focus and self-regulation help you consistently reach or work towards the goal. Ultimately, this comes across as dependability because people will see they can count on you to get things done.

Dependability

The hallmark of dependability is consistency and being consistent over time. As a leader, people are counting on you and therefore you need to be dependable.

In the context of self-leadership, dependability is coming to work on time, being available when you need to be and saying "yes" when you're asked to do something.

Of course, any characteristic, if taken to the extreme, can be overdone. Where dependability is concerned, it could conflict with your priorities. So, if dependability for you means that whatever work wants you to do, they can count on you to do it all the time, it might be that you're dependable at work, but then you have to question whether you're dependable at home as well.

I believe that leaders need to be aware of how to take care of themselves. If you give everything to your work or your company, there will be aspects of your personal life that don't work out so well. Ultimately this catches up with you and creates issues with your work.

As you move along your leadership journey, from leading yourself to leading teams to leading organizations, the demands on you increase as the responsibility increases. You have to make sure you take care of yourself and keep this in balance with other aspects of your life.

While dependability is certainly about saying "yes", it might also be about saying "no".

If you're aspiring to lead, or to lead more, it's important that you understand these qualities that people are looking for as they develop leaders and give them more responsibility. It really helps to keep these characteristics in mind when you're making decisions about how you go about your work day, or even how you go about your life.

We have talked about focus, self-discipline, and dependability in the context of self-leadership, but it's having a heart of service that will make all the difference as you move beyond self-leadership.

Service

Service isn't about taking on the role of a servant and becoming less, it is about taking on the role and being more. Serving yourself might feel good for the short term, but in the long run we find ourselves experiencing the greatest joy and the most satisfaction when we are serving others.

As you develop your skills as a self-leader, you will be working with other people. You will be living in a community with yourself, your co-workers, your family, your friends, and people you may never know. Opportunities to help others will abound and it is through serving others that you will learn much about yourself. I am not saying that you sacrifice yourself in service to others. In order for you to grow as a leader, it is important that your focus moves to those around you, how you impact them, how they impact you, and how you can work together to make a difference at work, at home, or in your community.

Focus on these characteristics to progress as a leader

In many businesses there is a strong focus on skills competence, which means often people who are best at a particular task seem to find their way into leading others to do that task. But once you want to move beyond this level of team leadership, and move along the continuum of leading bigger teams, leading departments and then leading organizations, it becomes essential to be aware of these characteristics.

If you aren't in a leadership position, but this is the direction in which you want to move, and you're struggling to get there, I would advise you to look not only at the elements we've discussed in this chapter, but also at the ones that come in the following chapters of Part 1.

Take some time to assess where you are in each of those elements. Chances are that if you're not progressing within leadership, and you can't seem to get past leading a very small team or feel stuck, you'll find the answers you're looking for within these characteristics. If you pay some attention to the characteristics discussed in Part 1 and work on those areas, you could well move past that sticking point because a lack of awareness in these areas is what's been holding you back.

"Leaders Worth Following are mentally tough and emotionally predictable. They are a rock for their people and the organization. They need to be tough as nails, but tender of heart."

The starting point for your leadership journey

Understanding motivation is really important. As I said earlier in the chapter, the same things don't motivate you every day and sometimes what inspires you to be effective one day won't be what inspires you to be effective the next. It is important that we are able to shift our thinking in order to keep ourselves optimally motivated. Looking for ways to create choice, connection and competence will help us maintain the best type of motivation. It is helpful to be able to shift your perspective and look at a situation through the lens of these optimal motivators.

By understanding your motivators and remembering what is important to you, you can consciously find the right motivation for each day. If you're not feeling particularly motivated, it could simply be that you're only focusing on one aspect of what motivates you. Having the ability to find, or create, the right motivation for yourself each day is an essential skill as a leader.

For example, imagine that it is important to make a good living for your family and one day you win the lottery or receive a windfall inheritance. All of a sudden, making a good living for your family isn't as urgent as it was before. If your only motivator is money, you have to consider what is important to you if money was no longer an issue. This is why being aware of creating choice, connection, and building competency is important for optimal motivation.

This is also why having that awareness about your various motivators is so important, because this allows you to pull those into play and shift your thinking to find the motivators that are the most compelling for you at any given point in time to inspire you to do your work.

The four characteristics I've talked about in this chapter – focus, self-regulation, dependability and service – are just the first characteristics you have to explore as you develop as a leader. All the characteristics we're going to explore in Part 1 build on each other.

Think of it like a continuum. We've started with focus, self-regulation, dependability and service. Next we're going to explore responsibility and independence. In Chapter 3, we'll dive into emotional control and self-esteem. Finally, as we finish Part 1, we'll come to critical thinking. Each one underpins the others and they are all equally important.

Mike's leadership lesson: Scouting

"Roger, my feet really hurt! I think I'm getting blisters…"

"Ahh, geez Jon, let's sit on this rock for a second and see if we can't do something about that! I remember getting blisters on my first hiking trip in the mountains so I know how sore your feet can be after a day of walking the trails," Roger said, rummaging in his pack looking for a Band-Aid.

"Won't we lose the others if we stop?"

"Don't you worry about that, I know where we're going and once we patch your feet up I'm sure we'll catch them easily," Roger said with a wink.

I'm sure there were many interactions like this between our two scout leaders, Roger and Chris, during our 50-mile hike in the Kiamichi Mountains in southeast Oklahoma. There were about 50 kids ranging in age from 12-17 that were participating and we were walking about 10 miles per day over five days. There was not a defined trail system as all the hiking was back country and we navigated with maps and compasses.

When I was younger, I was in scouting and felt drawn to leadership. At the time, I think my desire for leadership was about directing things towards what I wanted or what I thought was best. It was about me rather than serving others. I had a great time being a patrol leader and in organizing things I wanted to do. I felt like I was missing something and it was on this 50-mile hike that I saw something special in leadership.

Roger and Chris were always walking around mingling with the hikers. They had a sense of each person that was hiking and an idea of how they were doing. Everyone experienced fatigue, blisters, equipment issues, hunger, thirst, home sickness, and plenty more. Roger and Chris knew how to deal with all of these issues. They would let everyone know they had experienced similar challenges. They would explain what they did to deal with the various challenges. They could connect kids and suggest they buddy up, and oftentimes the kid who needed a pair of dry socks was buddied for the day with someone who brought too many socks.

Each morning, either Roger or Chris were missing when we all woke up and had breakfast. They would mysteriously reappear somewhere on the trail, usually around lunch. After we broke for lunch, one of them would always hang back to make sure our break area was returned to "normal". Even though we were trying to "take only pictures, and leave only footprints", 50 kids would leave a mess, even after they thought they had cleaned things up. Whoever hung back would usually arrive in camp an hour or more after the group made it in for the day. I found it interesting that they would have a few hikers with them.

Not quite a year after this experience, I had a conversation with Chris who told me that one of them would get up super early and essentially set the trail for the group. They were familiar with the route, but things could change since the last time they were on the trail. The lone hiker could cover much more ground than the group and they would hike as far as they could go in time to back track to meet for lunch. The person who hung back after lunch would invariably pick up stragglers and help them finish the day's hike. This process made sure every scout made it in and that the slowest scouts had just as much support as the quickest ones. Keep in mind that this was before the days of cell phones and "affordable" hand-held radios.

Leadership lessons...

The leaders who were on that scout trip exhibited all the qualities I've talked about in this chapter. They had focus to keep all of us scouts motivated and moving each day. They showed self-discipline in always being the first to rise and the last to go to bed. They were dependable. We all knew we could count on them to support us on that 50-mile hike.

Being a scout, of course, taught me to be prepared. Beyond that though, I learned that the best leaders are not always at the front of the pack. You will sometimes find them at the front, in the middle and at the back lending a helping hand and being of service to their co-workers, friends, family, and community.

Self-awareness and empathy: These traits got 50 scouts to complete (and mostly enjoy!) a 50-mile, back country hike. Possessing and demonstrating these traits will make you a leader worth following.

CHAPTER 2: GUIDING FORCES

"Responsibility and independence go hand-in-hand to propel a developing leader towards higher levels of leadership."

In the previous chapter, we talked about characteristics that set people apart and help them get ready for leadership. Guiding forces are also elements that set you apart, but I would describe these as an internal mechanism that helps keep you on the rails as you're starting to lead, rather than external qualities. There is some overlap here with self-discipline, but I believe there are two important guiding forces that will help set you apart and set you up for your leadership journey: responsibility and independence.

Responsibility

From a leadership perspective, the idea of responsibility is that you feel called to a higher level of accountability to both yourself and the people around you. This begins early in your leadership journey. It's exhibiting responsibility towards the things that are very close to you, which can include yourself, as well as your teammates.

As you progress along your leadership journey, by learning more about leading yourself, then leading teams and eventually leading organizations, that sphere of responsibility becomes bigger as your job changes.

People who are natural leaders will tend to step up and take responsibility when there's a job that needs to be done and everyone else is just standing around. When you're developing as a leader, you're the person who jumps in and takes personal responsibility, not only for doing things but also for the problems that come up.

Challenges or problems arise in projects and even in our day-to-day work. What sets someone who is on a leadership journey apart is that they will take responsibility for that problem and set about trying to fix it, rather than complaining about it or pointing fingers. This means they'll take action when they're faced with a challenging situation, rather than freezing or simply giving up and saying, "This is somebody else's problem, I can't do what I need to do." They'll take ownership of this challenge or problem and it will become theirs. Taking personal responsibility is an important quality of leadership.

While we can't change other people, or necessarily fix situations that belong to other people, someone who is a natural leader will assume they can do something. Even if they can't do everything, they will tackle the elements that they can. More often than not, that's enough to keep the project going or moving in the right direction.

Within the context of your leadership journey, responsibility means that you'll feel a personal responsibility to get something done or deal with a situation and you won't give up when you're faced with barriers. In fact, it's more than likely that you'll be the person figuring out how to overcome those barriers. Responsibility, in this sense, ties in closely with the second guiding force, independence.

Independence

Deciding to take responsibility for something is one thing, but you need to have a sense of independence or agency to empower you to think that you can actually take responsibility.

This is about not always relying upon others to solve the problem or find the answers to questions you may have. Early on in your career, when you're trying to figure things out, you might feel as though you have to go back to your supervisor for help. The difference when you have this guiding force of independence is that you're not going back to your supervisor about every question you have with a project. That doesn't demonstrate a high level of independence.

Instead, you're taking the approach that if you can't do everything, do something. You see yourself as empowered enough to take some action, even if there are elements in which you still need support.

There may be situations where you may not feel you have the authority to do something. In that case, you can approach your supervisor with options to solve the problem. After doing this a few times, your supervisor will most likely give you the room you need to make these decisions. Being able to take action, even when you are uncomfortable, is a sign of growing independence. Knowing what actions can be taken to get you closer to the end result is a sign of growing competence. It is important that you are aware of your own competence, and seek guidance when you are unsure about it, while at the same time growing your independence.

Combining responsibility with independence

Responsibility and independence go hand-in-hand to propel a developing leader towards higher levels of leadership. If you're part of a team, or just a sole worker, and you're able to demonstrate and use these guiding forces, you'll begin to build your competencies in these areas.

This is true whether you naturally take responsibility and feel that you have the autonomy to make things happen on your own, or whether you understand that these are important qualities to demonstrate and, therefore, look for opportunities to take responsibility and be independent. In my experience, when you start to do these things, you'll find people start seeing you as a natural leader and will turn to you to help move things along, organize and accomplish tasks.

Mike's leadership lesson: My first job

"Beep-beep-beep!" My hand reached out and hit the button on the alarm clock as I stretched and sat up. I didn't delay getting out of bed or feel tempted to fall back to sleep. I was excited to get up, start my day and get to work. You see, this was my first job and I had two choices: I could be at home chomping at the bit to go to work, or I could just go in.

I started my professional career straight out of college as a transmission design engineer at an electric cooperative that generated and transmitted electricity and sold that power to distribution cooperatives. When I started, I would always go to work early and I would tend to stay late.

When I say I'd go in early, I mean around 7am. I was in a brand new position and I was learning my job, so when I arrived in the morning I'd line up my day. I'd look at the projects I had and give myself time to wrap my head around the tasks that I needed to get done that day, or look at areas where I may have had problems or potential challenges.

By the time the other folks I worked with were starting their day, I was already into doing work. I always found it interesting that those people looked at me strangely and asked what I was doing at work so early. For me, it felt natural. I was taking responsibility for my work and ensuring that I knew what needed to be done and could do it.

When you're brand new in a position, you may not know everything that you need – I certainly didn't at that stage – and you can't be afraid to ask for help. I always found that coming in early and working independently gave me time to think things through. It also gave me time to line up the questions that I needed to ask my supervisor each day.

Because I had these questions ready, I was able to catch my supervisor first thing in the morning, before they got busy with their own stuff, sit down with them, run through my questions and then continue with my work. This helped to increase my competence and grow my independence. I took personal responsibility for my projects and worked on them as if they were my very own.

Leadership lessons...

If you look at supervisors who are doing a good job of leading teams, most of the time you'll notice that they come in a little bit earlier than their people. If you're aspiring to become a supervisor, and maybe lead teams, it's helpful to take on some of those habits that you see in other good supervisors, before you get to that position yourself.

Coming into work early to plan your day and spending a little bit of time later to tidy things up for the next day are two habits that manifest from these ideas of responsibility and independence.

Self-awareness: I knew I would learn more quickly and be better at my job if I had a little time to get organized and catch my supervisor first thing in the morning. Being aware of what you need to improve allows you to take responsibility for your own development.

How's your relationship with your work?

If you're passionate about your job and you're doing work that you believe in, it doesn't really feel like work. In this scenario, you get energy from working, rather than work taking energy from you.

However, especially as you progress in your career, some of the stressors and demands of the job can come at you, or the job doesn't feel like fun any more. When that happens, you can begin to resent what you're doing.

You might have been coming to work early, working hard and exercising these ideas of responsibility and independence. For a time, this has been giving you energy and helping you move along, but one day you show up to do that and you look around and see that other people aren't doing the same. This is when you may start to feel some resentment.

When this happens, there are two things that could be going on. The first is that you're right, other people aren't working as hard as you. The second is that you may have worked your energy levels too low. It could also be that there are now other priorities in your life that are competing for your time.

We all get that feeling of resentment from time to time, depending on where we are in our careers and our lives. The key is to sit with that feeling and understand it, rather than putting that feeling onto external factors. This is a sign for you to spend some time thinking about where you are.

There's a big discussion about work-life balance and what that looks like. I think you need to look at yourself as being in a relationship with your work. If you're in a relationship with another person, especially a serious relationship, it isn't going to be 50-50 all the time. Sometimes relationships are 90-10. Sometimes relationships are 10-90. Sometimes they are 50-50, but they ebb and flow depending on your partner's needs and what is going on in your life.

Your relationship with work is the same. Sometimes you're putting a lot into it, whether that's hours or energy – and those two aren't always the same. For me, the idea of work-life balance lies in understanding what priorities you have in your life, as well as at work, and being very, very true to them.

Hopefully, if you can spend some time thinking about those, you can find a way that your best self shows up for your life at work and that you know what you need to do to have your best self for your life when you're not at work. The word balance implies that these things have to be even, but I prefer to see it like a flow that shifts depending on what's going on.

Getting this right doesn't mean that you can't have some difficult times if you find that your personal life is really demanding at the same time that your professional life is demanding. When those two things line up, it can be really stressful because you don't feel like there's enough time in the day to deal with everything.

As a leader, you need to understand the ebb and flow of your relationship with your work early on, so that instead of running from any stress you encounter, you're able to understand where it's coming from and, therefore, deal with it rather than hiding from it.

In my experience, it's very common for stress to build up when you feel that there's a conflict between your work and personal lives. You feel as though there's not enough time to meet all the needs you have and that is where the stress comes from. Understanding this ebb and flow within the different areas of your life, and exploring what this idea of work-life balance really means, is important to enable you to cope with stress, in whatever form that shows up in your life. This is where our next concept, self-awareness, comes in.

A real-life story: My first CEO job

I mentioned earlier that I started as a transmission design engineer as my first job out of college, and I did that job for two years before my first professional leadership position opened up. I moved from that job after three years to work at a cooperative in Alaska. I worked there for 10 years and progressed in positions and leadership responsibility to the level of Chief Operating Officer, which I held when I left that organization. I have been in my current role as Chief Executive Officer (CEO) of a distribution cooperative for over 20 years. This was my first CEO position, and will most likely be my last. Thirty-eight years have passed since that day I showed up for work with my bright, shiny engineering diploma and started in that transmission design engineer position.

I have struggled with this idea of work-life balance for these 38 years, and I have made mistakes on both sides of that balance point while I searched for the solution to the equation: Work+Life=Balance. Unfortunately, my lived story is not a great example of how to find balance between work and life, it's more a story of what not to do.

It is easy now, as I look back over the past four decades, to see the times in my life where my balance was off and when the balance was spot on. It would be so easy to suggest that it was pressure, stress, someone, or something that took my balance away. The truth of the matter is that your balance comes from within you; and you, and you alone, are in charge of you. It is a matter of being true to yourself, but in order to do that you must know what your truths are. In the heat of the moment, we find ourselves being pulled by so many things and by so many relationships – the relationship with our significant other, the relationships with our family of origin, the relationships with our kids, friends, co-workers and so on. The truth I have discovered after all these years is that our relationship with ourselves is the first one we need to get right; otherwise, our giving to others – including our jobs – depletes us, creates internal conflicts, anxiety, and ultimately puts our life out of balance.

CHAPTER 3:
SELF-AWARENESS

"I believe that self-awareness helps you bring a better version of yourself to work, not just for you, but for the people around you."

There are several elements that sit under the context of self-awareness. However, it's important to understand that if you want to be an effective leader, you have to be self-aware of your emotions and how you feel about yourself.

An aspiring leader would do very well to understand how they are feeling about things, but it's an area many people neglect. We can be very tone-deaf to our own internal feelings. For a lot of us, it seems as though society teaches us that feelings are bad. We're not supposed to feel mad or angry, hurt or sad. As a result, we tend to stuff those feelings away or act like they're not there.

This process works until it doesn't. People are made to feel, and when we shut down feelings that we don't like, we pay the price of shutting down the other feelings as well. Feelings are messy, scary, and complicated, but they give us information if we use the rational part of the brain, our prefrontal cortex, to understand and keep in check that small part of our brain called the amygdala, which is the main source of our emotional response and our fight-or-flight reaction. If you are under stress, there is a good chance you have a stress hormone called cortisol in your system. It turns out that cortisol actually turns off your rational thinking by inhibiting the functioning of your prefrontal cortex.

However, if you can recognize your feelings and name them, you can remove the power these feelings have over you – whether you're feeling afraid, anxious or angry – and prevent yourself from experiencing the anxiety these feelings provoke. Recognizing and naming your feelings is the first step to becoming self-aware and developing emotional awareness and control.

We can't control what we don't understand. If you don't know what anxiety is and what that feels like, you may not even realize that you're under stress and feeling anxious. The funny thing is that the people around you, the ones walking on eggshells, feel your mood and your anxiety for you.

In the last chapter, I talked about the idea of work+life=balance, where the two ebb and flow in such a way that you feel balanced. However, when we find ourselves with competing priorities and we're wondering how we can get everything done, we often start to worry. That's when the stress comes in, which is the mental aspect of the situation. The way I look at it is that anxiety is the physical manifestation of that stress in your body. It's that physical feeling in your gut.

The first aspect of self-awareness is being able to identify how you're being impacted by situations. That's really important, because if you can say, "That's a weird feeling, where is this coming from, why is this happening to me?" then you have a chance of being able to bring that into perspective and deal with it. This is you purposefully engaging your rational thinking by turning on your prefrontal cortex to push back on the emotional reactions your amygdala is cooking up for you.

This isn't just important for you. If something is bothering you, has upset you or is really challenging you, it can create energy in your body which can sometimes be negative. If you don't know how to deal with that energy, it can end up leaking out onto other people, which will ruin your effectiveness as a leader.

We've all experienced situations where that energy does leak out onto our friends, family or the people at work; and those are not shining moments of self-leadership. But if you don't know that's happening to you then you don't have much of a chance of resolving it.

Emotional control

The idea of emotional control is to sense that you have these feelings and name them. Maybe you're frustrated with somebody and if you're able to say, "I'm feeling frustrated right now", that's a good thing because you have a chance of dealing with it. However, if you're blind to that feeling and don't know what it is then it can leak out in other ways and impact other people.

The other aspect of emotional control is being able to manage your emotions. You start by understanding that you have feelings and then you use those feelings to diagnose yourself or what might be bothering you. This allows you to figure out a positive way to resolve the situation. That's emotional control.

You recognize your feelings about a situation, understand what's driving them, think of the best path forward and then follow it. When you're able to do this, you'll be seen as a person who is even and predictable.

Of course, if someone never shows any emotion you might wonder about that; but what you're aiming for with emotional control is to think about how and when you show your emotions to others. When this is done well, it makes you predictable to others. This is what you want to be as a leader. We've all had a boss or coworker that everyone tiptoes around on eggshells, because we've been afraid of setting them off. That's not the sign of someone who's predictable and has emotional control.

Having self-awareness of what's going on inside of you, as well as understanding your impact on the people around you, is all part of the emotional control you need to develop on your leadership journey. Knowing your impact on others, on your team and on your organization – and being concerned about that – is a sign of a person who is capable of leading more than just themselves.

Ultimately, I believe that self-awareness helps you bring a better version of yourself to work, not just for you, but for the people around you.

"Leaders Worth Following own their weaknesses and know how to ask for help."

Transitioning from self-awareness to emotional control

Self-awareness begins with the understanding that you have feelings and that you understand what those are, whether you're mad, happy, sad or depressed on any given day. The next stage is being able to sit with those feelings and find out where they're coming from. You have to name those feelings and then figure out how you're going to move forward in that moment or that day, with those feelings, in a way that's beneficial to you and the people around you. The decision about how you move forward is emotional control.

Now, because we're human, we're not always going to be good at that. We are going to have days where, for whatever reason, we're better at it than others. What we have to be able to do is look at ourselves when we're exercising self-awareness and emotional control, and be honest about how we have done well with that and where we could maybe improve. This ties into the next element of self-awareness, which is self-esteem.

Self-esteem aka Self-love

The concept of self-esteem is that people have confidence in themselves so that even when they make mistakes, they care enough about themselves to forgive themselves for the mistake. They recognize that they took a particular action and wish they had done better, but then they are able to forgive themselves for what happened, and forgive themselves if they exhibited a lack of emotional control. Another aspect of self-esteem is having the confidence to approach others and make an apology.

Guilt vs. shame

The difference between guilt and shame is a topic that's often discussed and Brené Brown, in her book *Daring Greatly*[2], provides a great description of the difference between guilt and shame. Guilt is a feeling, so you know that you did something wrong, whereas shame is the feeling that something is wrong with you. Put simply, it's the difference between: *I did something bad* and *I am bad.*

Having self-esteem allows you to use that feeling of guilt to self-correct and make amends. However, if you don't have high self-esteem, those feelings turn to shame and shame does not disclose, it hides. You hide it from yourself and you certainly hide it from other people.

The concept of self-awareness is ultimately underpinned by this idea of self-esteem, which is to have enough confidence in yourself to forgive yourself for what you did and not let those problems become shame,

2 Brene Brown, (2015), *Daring Greatly: How the Courage to be Vulnerable Transforms the Way We Live, Love, Parent and Lead*, Penguin Life

which is something you hide and don't talk about. Feelings of shame can really erode the whole process of being self-aware and prevent us from growing as a person and a leader as a result.

How to develop your self-awareness

First of all, nobody is going to be perfect at this. We are all going to have moments where we nail it and are able to self regulate and come through with an ideal outcome. We're also all going to have moments where we get negative outcomes from a situation.

However, if you have noticed you are getting more negative than positive outcomes from your interactions with others, and you want to make a change, then the first thing you should do is congratulate yourself, because the first step is simply being aware of that desire and making that choice.

When you have this level of self-awareness and you're able to think about events and interactions in the context that they work together as a system, you will have an opportunity to make changes that lead to more positive outcomes.

It's also important to recognize that we all cope with situations differently. If we take the Covid-19 pandemic that we've all experienced (at the time of writing, very recently!), that's an external stressor that nobody can run from. Everybody has experienced the stress of the pandemic, but we've also all experienced it differently.

Part of self-awareness is understanding what you're feeling and how that affects your reactions. But it's also about considering how we handle stress and acknowledging that we all have different mechanisms for coping with it.

There are lots of techniques out there for calming yourself and becoming more mindful. Being too hungry or too tired are probably the biggest things that weaken us, so having the self-awareness to recognize when we are super hungry or super tired is important. This is about taking care of your body. Make sure you're getting enough sleep, doing physical activity and putting the right things in your body. Your personal resilience has a lot to do with how you take care of yourself.

The earlier in your leadership journey you can learn the importance of self-care, the more benefits you will see from it. Being self-aware enough to see how these factors – sleep, physical fitness and diet – are connected and how they drive outcomes for you is essential, as a leader or an aspiring leader. The sooner you recognize this, the better your leadership journey will be not only for you, but for the people around you.

Over my life, I've seen lots of examples where people have made unhealthy choices to help them cope with their stress, and in the end they pay the price for that.

You can also ask for help and open yourself up to some trusted people in your life or at work. These people will help you, give you some feedback and encourage you if you go to them and explain that you want to work on your self-awareness as part of your leadership journey.

Walking on eggshells

When you have someone on a team, either as a team member or a team leader, who is unable to exercise self-awareness and emotional control, the experience for that team is very painful. Often these teams don't function well and there's some discomfort. Depending on how that team is put together, it can get to the point of being very dysfunctional, where people feel like they're walking on eggshells when they're together.

Obviously, every member of the team is there to serve the team and ultimately accomplish the goal, but the dysfunction and walking on eggshells creates a really bad environment.

Mike's leadership lesson: Dan, Al and Helen

Dan, Al and Helen had been working together for months, but there was always an underlying tension between the three of them.

As the engineer leading the project, Dan was always pushing everyone to do more. He was very aware of their deadlines and wanted to make sure the job was done well and on schedule. The deadlines were tight but they were doable, if everyone pulled their weight and made a few sacrifices. Dan was so focused on his work and hitting the project deadlines, he didn't stop to think about how his approach might make Al and Helen feel.

Al's speciality was communications, while Helen was a business generalist. Over the course of the project, the two had become friends, a bond largely formed due to Dan's overly pushy approach. The two had been complaining about the way he was pushing the team for months, usually on a coffee break or via the odd private message or two.

However, as the deadline got closer and Dan pushed ever harder, Helen and Al spent more and more time complaining about how hard he was expecting them to work. "Doesn't he realize there's more to life than work?" Al quipped one day, to which Helen replied, "Clearly his life is his work, otherwise why would he push so hard?"

Tensions were bubbling beneath the surface for weeks, with Al and Helen feeling increasingly marginalized by Dan's approach. In meetings, he didn't seem to care what their opinions were or, at times, even give the illusion of listening to them.

During one particularly stressful phone meeting, where the three of them were trying to fix a specific problem, Al pinged Helen a message, "Do you even think there's any point in us being here? He may as well be talking to two mannequins for all the notice he's taking of us." "I know! I wonder what the point of having these meetings is when he'll just go off and do what he wants anyway," Helen replied.

"Is it just me, or is his voice sounding even more annoying than usual today?" "I try to zone it out, treat it like white noise." "Teach me how! This man has an uncanny ability to make me want to punch a wall!" "Or him?"... And so the exchange continued, becoming more and more personal.

Dan saw the messages start pinging up on his phone about 15 minutes into the meeting. Initially he ignored them, but as they became more and more barbed, it rankled him. He put his phone out of sight, tried to continue talking, pretending he hadn't seen them, but they were niggling.

Eventually he paused, "Al, if you want to punch me, I'd rather you came and talked to me about it than sending messages to

Helen while we're on a call." Dead silence met his comment at the other end of the line.

"Punch you...?" stammered Al, "What makes you think I'd want to do that?" he asked hesitantly, although he already knew the answer. A quick glance at the messages showed him that he'd started his exchange with Helen in the group chat that the three of them shared for work, rather than their private chat. Helen too was realizing their mistake and cursing under her breath.

Dan ended the meeting with, "I can't talk to the two of you after this, let alone work with you." Of course, he reported the incident to senior management. It was clear very quickly that mitigation was not an option in this situation, so the team was disbanded and new people were assembled to complete the project that Dan, Al and Helen had started.

Leadership lessons...

We can all struggle to get along with our colleagues from time to time, but the way that Al and Helen behaved was inexcusable. In fact, the two of them felt a great deal of embarrassment and shame about their conduct. They knew that they had crossed a line in how they were talking, even if the messages had accidentally been sent to Dan.

For his part, Dan was obviously hurt by the comments he saw, but the end result wasn't entirely negative. He had something of an epiphany and realized that he needed to change the way he led and worked. What Al and Helen were unaware of was that Dan was already receiving coaching to help him become less intensely driven and more accommodating to the people on his teams. However, when Dan saw their comments pinging up on his phone, everything he'd been working on became painfully real and seemingly overwhelming.

Do you think all three of these people would have continued to work at the same organization in the long term, even if they were now on separate teams? From my experience of similar incidents, people involved in this kind of issue tend to go their separate ways. They might not all leave at the same time, but being involved in this kind of egregious incident often prompts them to look for work elsewhere.

As an organization, that may mean you lose high-performing, high-potential employees, all due to a lack of self-awareness that creates this kind of dysfunction within a team.

How can you prevent similar incidents from happening in the future if this is a concern at your organization? My advice is to develop a leadership and training program that helps people address these issues and develop their self-awareness to prevent similar situations arising at your firm.

Self-awareness: You have to consider how your behavior might affect others you're working with or leading. If you aren't aware, you won't realize there's a problem that needs to be addressed until it's too late.

Encouraging self-awareness and emotional control

That story is one example of the many things that made us, as an organization, formalize this idea of helping leaders understand what self-leadership looks like, what taking leadership looks like and what organizational leadership looks like. Encouraging people at every level to develop self-awareness and emotional control involves training and development to help them improve, and it means setting out the expectations and outcomes.

There isn't a curriculum for self-awareness; however, what we developed was a process for enabling discussions around this topic. It's having conversations about what it takes to become a good leader, and talking about what comes up. This is all part of a wider process that involves everyone in the business talking about issues, challenges and opportunities.

CHAPTER 4: EVALUATOR/ JUDGMENT

"Critical thinking is developed through experience, learning, and understanding the relationship between things."

In this final chapter of Part 1, we're going to explore critical thinking in the context of leading yourself and leading others. Being able to evaluate situations and make decisions is a crucial part of being a self-leader, as well as a team or organizational leader.

We've already looked at motivators, which are the things that keep you moving in the direction you want to go and remembering what you want. This encompasses the concepts of being dependable, showing up and being reliable. Then we explored guiding forces, where you take responsibility for things. You see problems or challenges as something of which you can take ownership. You look for places where you can make a change in what you're doing, rather than worrying about what you can't do. You find ways of making progress in the areas you control.

In the last chapter, we looked at self-awareness, which means being aware of your feelings and using them to make decisions about how you're going to interface with yourself and with others, that works to create the most positive outcomes.

Critical thinking begins here because it relates to you, and is the ability to pull all of these things together to make decisions about how you're going to present yourself to your team and your coworkers, as well as to make decisions for yourself.

Critical thinking

At its simplest, critical thinking is being able to synthesize all the information and knowledge that you have into assumptions. You then take those assumptions and you make a decision. If you're good at critical thinking, the decisions that you make are the right ones. If you're not good at critical thinking, the decisions you make aren't the right ones, because the assumptions you made were not the best assumptions.

As I said, critical thinking is the ability to pull your motivators, guiding forces and self-awareness together, and to end up with the best "most right" decisions. This is really important because if you can't get to the best "most right" decisions, leading yourself and leading others is going to be a real challenge. I use the term "most right" decision as a way to emphasize that most complex decisions involve trade-offs. Problems like math problems typically have a correct answer, but as you move more into leadership, many of the decisions you make don't have just one answer. This is where critical thinking comes in.

As a process, critical thinking involves walking through the various data points you have for a particular decision, and reaching the best conclusion you can. Critical thinking is developed through experience, learning, and understanding the relationship between things, i.e. "connecting the dots".

A process of continual learning

It is also a skill that develops over time. Your ability to take all the data and information you have available to you, and think about what could be the best path forward for you, improves with experience.

For instance, you're in a position where you need to communicate something to people about a particular situation. You have the option to send people an email or pull everybody together on a Zoom call and have a conversation. You pick the email over the Zoom call, but the email you send has a different meaning to every person who reads it because they filter your words based on their perception. At the end of the day, you realize that having a Zoom call would have been a better way to handle it.

If you are learning and developing your critical thinking, when you find yourself in that scenario again, you'll analyze the data you have about whether to send an email or hold a video conference, and you'll decide to do a video conference. You've learned from sending that email, which didn't work out well, and you've improved your critical thinking as a result.

As you're leading yourself early in your career, you will always be working through this process of thinking, 'Here's my data and the information I have at hand, here are my assumptions and here's what I'm going to do.' Early in your journey as a leader, your process will be very rigorous. You'll go through these steps every time. You'll learn from those outcomes and the next time it happens, you'll still go through the steps and still get to the decision, but hopefully you'll have learned what leads to better outcomes.

Critical thinking is essential for leadership

There are some people who can't follow this critical thinking process. These people will not find themselves in leadership positions if they can't learn from past mistakes; nor will they be able to move themselves along a leadership journey.

However, those who are good at critical thinking are able to progress on their leadership journey. If you look ahead on the leadership journey to someone who is a very capable and experienced leader, who has led organizations for a long time, you'll find that they don't go through the same rigorous process any more.

That's because our brains work with pattern recognition, and the more experience you get, the more you're able to see patterns in information and situations, and instinctively know what is the best "most right" decision.

I remember going through this process of critical thinking for years in the earlier part of my leadership career and I know it takes mental energy to do that. There are lots of ways you can line up all your assumptions to reach a decision. I've been a CEO for over 20 years and I can remember how taxing it was to make decisions and think through situations. I even remember thinking, about five years into my job as CEO, that I would be lucky to last another five years.

Around the 10-year mark, something changed. All of a sudden, this rigor and discipline behind my thinking became much easier; and when I was making decisions, I just knew what to do without having to go through this big process. That was because I had practiced this process and developed these patterns in the way I think about problem solving and decision making.

In self-leadership, you're learning this process of laying everything out to get to decisions and you're learning from the decisions you make. Leaders who are able to move from self-leadership to team leadership have this ability. When you have built a pattern of applying this process and making good decisions, you're ready to move to the next level of leadership.

When you get to team leadership, you have to follow the same process but the topics are more complex. Because you're leading a team, your decision making isn't just for you any more, it's for all the people in your team too. As you progress from team leadership to organizational leadership, the complexity increases again.

All of this starts by developing your critical thinking as a self-leader. You need to begin here, gain experience, and gradually work up to more complex situations and decision making.

Mike's leadership lesson: Carl and Tim

I've had many leaders throughout my career, some have been good and some have been bad. The worst leader I have ever personally experienced took the job to make his "high five". He came into his job with the idea that he would be served by his job. He was driven to get things done; not for the good of his company, but for his own pride and ego. Carl would not take the time to sit with the resistance he might be feeling from others; instead, he would lash out, personalize everything and assume the victim role. Carl would drink, tell people off and then apologize the next day. He was unpredictable and had no clue of his impact on others. He saw the organization and its people as being of service to him. In the end, he left a large amount of organizational carnage in his wake which took years to work through.

By contrast, I had another leader called Tim who had very high emotional intelligence. Tim could read people as well as be analytical. He used his feelings, or his gut, and his intellect to make decisions. Tim was the consummate negotiator and was able to renegotiate seemingly ironclad contracts with large corporations that had no incentive or reason to renegotiate. His skills saved his co-op millions in excessive costs and changed the "old way" of doing business. Kenny Rogers has a song called *The Gambler* with the line, "You have to know when to hold 'em, know when to fold 'em, know when to walk away, know when to run." This is a great real-life example of emotional control, self-awareness, and critical thinking.

Leadership lessons...

What I learned from Carl, the bad leader, was the importance of sitting with your discomfort in order to understand what it may be trying to teach you. Good leaders will sleep on difficult decisions, rather than being rash and having to apologize the next day. The wake that a bad leader makes is something the organization pays for – for a long time.

What I learned from Tim was that good leaders trust their gut and their mind. He also showed me the value of emotional intelligence in a leadership role. Understanding others is important, but you have to first understand yourself.

It is really easy to take your feelings of worry, anxiety, fear, and uncertainty and to project them onto other people, especially if you are not spending the time to understand yourself. Being able to understand others is critical for good leadership, yet the challenge is that you have to understand yourself first. Your ability to think and process external information relies on your ability to understand yourself.

Ego and empathy: As a leader, you have to be able to see past your own ego to understand and empathize with others; otherwise, you are likely to make poor decisions and hurt people along the way.

How to develop your critical thinking skills

You have to begin with an understanding of the concept of connecting everything to make a decision. I think it's very helpful to make your process visual and, in my experience, we tend to do this instinctively by making lists or mind maps. Mind maps are a particularly easy way to visualize your decision-making process, showing how things link together and lead to outcomes.

Collaborating with other people is also useful for developing your critical thinking. Getting everyone in a room together (or an online meeting space these days) and whiteboarding a particular issue, walking through the scenarios, is really important. Using whiteboards, either in person or virtually, is a good process for collaborative decision making. As a self-leader, you can collaborate with coworkers whom you know and trust. You might start by following this process yourself, and then bring in just one coworker.

Hopefully, if you're in an organization that understands the process of developing leaders, your supervisor or team leader will be running collaborative decision-making sessions like this and you'll see that model and be able to recognize it for the opportunity that it is.

Even without intention, this will often happen to varying degrees in any organization because it's just the way humans work together. If you're aware of this, you can tune into those situations and recognize them as opportunities to develop your critical thinking.

The building blocks for self-management and self-focus

All four of the aspects that we've talked about as part of self-management – the motivators, the guiding forces, self-awareness and the evaluator – are independent, but they work together to position you to become a really good self-leader and a really great coworker. Becoming good at applying these in your everyday work life positions you to take the next steps on your leadership journey.

This means moving into leading teams and applying the same skills, but maybe applying them to different situations and to challenges and opportunities with increased complexity.

Now that you've made it through the ideas and concepts of being a great self-leader and a great team member, it's time to focus on scaling those up and looking at them from multiple directions and multiple perspectives, and really understanding what it's going to take to become a really great leader of teams.

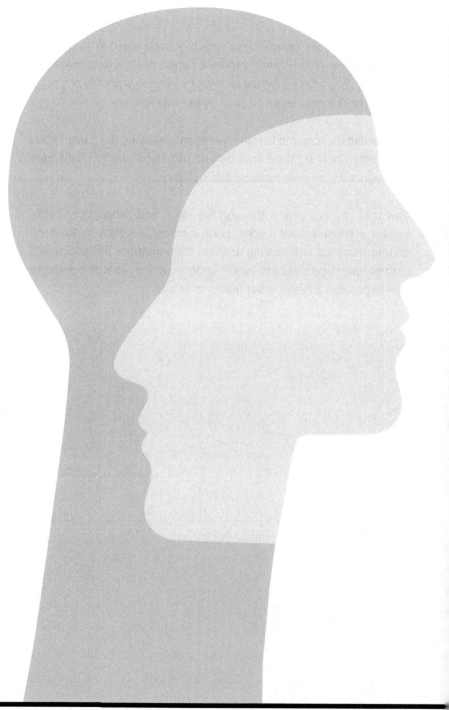

PART 2:

Interpersonal Ability/Team Focus

As you move from self-leadership to leading teams, your interpersonal ability becomes more important. This is about your awareness of your impact on the people around you and your ability to motivate and inspire others to focus their efforts on what the team is trying to accomplish.

There are many ways to look at interpersonal ability, and a person's ability to influence people. Someone could be very passionate about a topic or a goal and by sharing their passion they inspire others to feel that passion. Some people just have that natural charisma and others are drawn to their energy and want to be part of it.

However you view interpersonal ability, the big step is recognizing it in yourself. If you're observing and developing leaders, then it's also recognizing the people who can bring the energy of others and their focus to bear on goals that will be best accomplished through a team effort.

In the first part of this book, we explored self-leadership. When you're working on self-leadership, your goals, tasks and everything you're doing is very specific. However, as you start to move into team leadership, the complexity of the challenges and goals that you're working on become more than one person can do.

This is why you need to understand the importance of teams. You'll need to leverage different expertise and different perspectives on problems or challenges to accomplish goals. Your ability to lead in these more complex situations all begins with your ability to work well with others and to lead teams.

CHAPTER 5: UNDERSTANDING YOUR WAKE

"It's really important to understand what it's like for people to be led by you, and to understand what impact you have on other people."

When I talk about understanding your wake, I find the easiest analogy to understand is that of a boat. Imagine that you're driving a boat across a calm lake. As you move through the water, the engine creates a wake. How big and how turbulent that is will depend on how fast you're going and the way in which you're handling the boat.

Now imagine that someone is trying to waterski behind your boat. If your wake is too turbulent, that's going to be very challenging for them. You can also see that the ripples of your wake reach much further than just the water behind your boat, as I explained in Chapter 1.

We all have a wake, but when you are aware of it and understand your wake, hopefully you'll look back and you won't see chaos behind you.

Mike's leadership lesson: George Bush (and broccoli)

"I do not like broccoli. And I haven't liked it since I was a little kid and my mother made me eat it. And I'm president of the United States, and I'm not going to eat any more broccoli!"[3]

Those words, spoken by George H.W. Bush during his presidency, had more of an impact than he likely imagined. By talking negatively about broccoli, he created a huge dent in the industry. People even stopped eating broccoli because the president had said he didn't like it. All the broccoli producers were upset because he was hurting their business.

This might be a story that you've heard before, but maybe not. Either way, it includes some important lessons around being aware of your wake.

Leadership lessons...

If you don't see your wake and how it affects other people, then you won't be sensitive to those 'broccoli' moments you might have as a leader.

3 (1990), 'I'm President, So No More Broccoli!', *New York Times,* 23 March, Section A, Page 14 of the national edition, available at: https://www.nytimes.com/1990/03/23/us/i-m-president-so-no-more-broccoli.html

As a leader, if you're sensitive to your ego and dinero, people will be more willing to give you the discretionary effort you need to help your company be successful. They will meet you with their best energy and their best selves to work to overcome challenges in the organization. Encouraging this effort involves taking a more egalitarian approach to leadership where you don't always have to be the best at everything, you don't have to make the most money and you don't need to have the best parking spot.

Over the years, I've watched ego take people down because they couldn't admit they were wrong, or they made a bad decision and blamed it on someone else.

When it comes to dinero, you often see leaders of struggling organizations letting everyone else take pay cuts while they still take home a large salary and bonuses. It's particularly endemic in bankruptcies, where the executives' bonus plans somehow seem to survive the bankruptcy. If you look at most bankruptcies, you'll find an article somewhere about how the top leadership is still getting paid big money while everyone else in the company is suffering. The way I look at leadership, that definitely falls into the No-Os.

Ego and dinero: When you fail to consider your wake as a leader, it's much easier to fall into the traps of the No-Os. You have to think carefully about whether your actions or words could have a negative impact on others.

As a leader, it's really important to understand what it's like for people to be led by you, and to understand what impact you have on other people. The first stage lies with the understanding that you do have an impact on those around you. However, you need to take this further and make sure that the people who experience you and those you lead will find it very easy to follow you.

There are several areas that you can develop to really understand your wake, and we're going to talk about the three most important of these in this chapter: objectivity, listening, and being sensitive to others.

"Leaders Worth Following have great expectations and an even greater heart."

Objectivity

Objectivity, begins with keeping an open mind. When you're beginning to lead teams, you'll be bringing other people's expertise and experiences to bear on solving a problem or accomplishing a goal. To do this, you have to be objective. If, however, you have already decided what needs to happen and where things are going, then you haven't left any room for the people around you to contribute and take ownership of the situation.

Obviously we all have thoughts and opinions on where things need to go and how they should be done. That's okay, but where you can get into trouble as a leader, especially when your leadership is formally recognized, is when you're in a situation where it feels like everybody in the room is waiting for you to tell them what to do or make a decision about where things should go.

In some situations, this approach can work really well, provided you're very familiar with what's going on. However, the problem that you run into when you lead in this way is that your team's work and output will only be as good as you. That may work for a while, but as you get better at leading teams, you'll be assigned more and more complex problems. This is when objectivity becomes crucial.

At this point, there is a strong need for you, as the leader, to be objective. You have to suspend your thoughts, desires and opinions and invite other people to contribute and give their perspectives. To me, this is objectivity in leadership; putting aside your thoughts and opinions on how to solve a problem and getting feedback from your team.

When you listen to your team's thoughts and opinions, not only will it help them feel more engaged and make them want to contribute more to what's going on, but it will also improve the results you get. My experience has shown that when you're able to take that step back and adopt objectivity, the results are much greater than if you just tell people what to do.

As a newly appointed leader or supervisor, there might be a temptation to do things your way and while you can do that, this is a short-sighted approach to take. Ultimately, your role as a team leader is to bring that team together and to get the best out of everybody to identify and solve a problem or to make whatever your team is tasked with.

The majority of the time, I think it really is important for the leader to set aside their ideas and get this feedback from their team about what needs to happen. However, there are urgent situations, or perhaps a crisis, when a leader taking a more directive approach becomes important. It could also be that your team members are relatively inexperienced and this can be another scenario where you need to be more directive as a leader.

Even if this is the case, there is a saying that is worth remembering: "If you want to learn how not to do something, call an expert." The value of a team doesn't just lie in their experience. The value of a beginner's mind is really important in problem solving too. When you can be objective and give everyone the opportunity to share their feedback, you will likely find some good ideas, because the people in your team may not have convinced themselves that the problem can't be solved in a certain way.

What I'm talking about here is leaders cultivating a mindset of objectivity, where they are able to suspend their thoughts and inclinations to make room for others to contribute. This links very closely with the next area we're going to explore: listening.

Listening

When a leader has that objectivity mindset, which means they keep an open mind, there is a true willingness within them to hear what other people have to say and to take that to heart. This mindset is internal, but the external way that you show your objectivity to people is by really listening to them.

I think we've all been in meetings where we're talking to somebody and it's obvious that their focus is someplace else. I've certainly been in meetings where we've had a team assembled to work on solving a problem or a challenge, so there's some dialogue happening; but when you look around you realize that when some people aren't talking, they're focusing on something else, such as looking at their screen or typing an email. Some of that might be relevant to what's going on, but more often it's a sign that someone isn't really listening.

If you're going to listen to people as a leader, you need to be present to them, whether you're listening as a group or one-to-one. The ability to be a good listener is essential for leading teams.

Mike's leadership lesson: The importance of listening

"Hi Mike, what's going on? What's the problem?" Paul barely looked up from the mountain of paperwork in front of him and continued writing as I was speaking. I continued talking, noticing that he wasn't taking notes about what I was saying but that he was doing his paperwork. I paused and he looked up at me over his glasses and said, "You don't mind if I sign this paperwork while you're talking, do you?"

What could I say except, "Of course not." This interaction happened early in my career. Paul was my supervisor and I'd gone to talk to him about a challenge I was having. In that situation, it's a bad question because most people aren't going to tell their supervisor off (I certainly didn't). I kept talking, but I was aware he wasn't really listening to me.

Leadership lessons...

The right thing for my supervisor to have done in that situation would have been to set down his pen and listen to me talk about my problem. But in asking me that leading question, he was banking on my politeness and knew that with the power differential between us, I wouldn't say, "Yes, I mind."

However, I would say that someone who has the courage to ask their supervisor to put down their pen is probably someone worth listening to.

I'd also like to add that I believe taking notes when you're listening to someone is important. Jotting things down that are related to what they're saying can help you show people that you're actually listening to them.

Listening is about keeping yourself fully engaged. As the receiver of information, there are lots of ways you can do that and taking some really quick notes and jotting your thoughts down is just one of them.

Ego: You have to think about the other person and how they will feel in all your interactions as a leader. When you only consider yourself, you're letting your ego take over.

Active listening skills

Most of us understand basic active listening skills, but as a leader it's important to make sure you're using them with your team. They can involve paraphrasing what the other person is saying to you, so that they are hearing that you've understood them. Restating ideas or points back to them can be helpful too. Asking questions to clarify points is another important element of active listening.

But I think the most important one is to look at people and make eye contact with them while they're speaking. Your body language is also really important, because when your body language is consistent with theirs it demonstrates that you're really listening. This doesn't have to be complicated, it's simply a case of mirroring how they're positioning the parts of their body, whether that's crossing their arms or clasping their hands together.

Mirroring someone's body language creates a sense of comfort for the person speaking and invites them into a deeper conversation because it shows that you're paying attention.

There is some body language that all of us understand. For instance, if you start talking to someone and they cross their arms and close themselves off, you're going to get the sense that they really don't want to listen to you.

Another tip to show someone that you're really listening to them is to physically show that you're putting aside what you're currently doing in order to pay attention to them. If you have an office, that could be coming out from behind your desk and sitting at a conference table with them. It might be as simple as closing your laptop or turning off your computer so that you can be more present with that person. This whole concept of active listening is about finding ways that you can reduce the barriers between you and the other person as they try to talk and as you try to listen.

Communicating in a virtual world

With the Covid-19 pandemic and the rapid change to more virtual working environments, leaders have had to adapt quickly.

One thing I noticed among my team leads was that the ones who are really instinctive and natural leaders very quickly increased the frequency with which they were communicating with everyone on their teams.

Before the pandemic, they would maybe have a longer weekly conversation with each person to check in, or a face-to-face chat every couple of days. But in the virtual world, they very quickly made the effort to have a face-to-face call with their folks twice a day. These were just short, quick conversations throughout the day, but they were impactful and a way to keep connected to their people, as well as make themselves available.

Leaders also need to be aware of the signals that they might be sending out to their team about their willingness to listen and be available in a virtual environment. A lot of the software that we use allows us to see whether the other person is busy or not before we call them because we can see their calendar. However, I'm not sure that's such a great idea, because it puts up a barrier that might prevent people from reaching out to you.

It might help to consider this as your virtual wake. When you set up calendar items where you're 'busy' and your diary is full of appointments and 'red' blocks of time, it can give the appearance that you're not available for your team. When you're collaborating virtually, it's important to be aware of what kind of signals you're sending out about your availability and willingness to visit with your team. This links in with the final point related to understanding your wake: being sensitive to others.

Being sensitive to others

Sensitivity as a leader is your ability to understand how your people are feeling and it really helps you to develop empathy with them. I think a lot of people confuse empathy and sympathy. Brené Brown describes the difference between empathy and sympathy with a story about someone falling down a well.

You fall into a well and you're trapped at the bottom. The person who has sympathy for you looks over the top of the well and says, "Man you're in a well, that really sucks, that's not good." The person who has empathy for you jumps into the well to keep you company and supports you as you find your way out.[4]

When it comes to sensitivity to others, leaders need to be able to meet people where they are and understand what they're going through. So when people come to you as a leader, with problems or challenges, you can't be afraid to feel what they're feeling and join them in their struggle, whether that's frustration at work or other things that are going on.

We all try to bring our best selves to work, but the reality is that when you come to work you bring everything with you. That means if you're having a bad day at home, you're potentially going to be having a bad day at work. It also means that if you have a bad day at work, you might have a bad evening at home when you leave. Even though we try to keep these things separate, we don't always succeed.

As a leader you need to be able to understand what other people are going through, whether that's things that are going on in their own lives or, in the context of understanding your wake, understanding how your behavior impacts others.

If you're doing things that are making people uncomfortable and you're totally blind to that, you're probably not going to get very far as a leader of teams. Having awareness of how other people are feeling and understanding people's emotions are essential if you want to move on from leading a team to leading multiple teams within an organization.

4 Brené Brown (2013), *Brené Brown on Empathy*, RSA, 10 December, available at: https://www. thersa.org/video/shorts/2013/12/brene-brown-on-empathy

Having an ability to understand people's emotions and where they're coming from is the mark of an authentic leader.

Understanding your wake

Understanding your wake and your impact on others means that you're prepared to look behind your speedboat and see what your wake is doing.

If you don't have objectivity and aren't willing to accept that other people's ideas might be good too; if you don't have the capacity to listen to people; and if you're not sensitive to the outcome of situations or your impacts on them, their impacts on each other and the effect that has on getting the job done, then you're the guy in the speedboat who's driving too fast, creating a huge wake and knocking people over. That's a sign of an ego and, potentially, also a libido or dinero leadership failure.

You never look back and you think life is great, but if you just took a moment to look behind you then you'd see the havoc that you're creating. Failing to pay attention to, and understand your wake is the risk that you take if you don't develop a mindset of objectivity, actively listen to people, and display sensitivity for others.

"Leaders must understand what it feels like to live in their wake."

In the long term, it's much easier if you are aware of the wake that you leave and in order to do that you need to embody the qualities

I've talked about in this chapter. Be objective, listen to others and care about how others feel. Be aware of what's going on with other people each day, as well as how they're being impacted by what you're asking them to do and how you're asking them to do it.

I can tell you that there was a time in my career when I didn't care about my wake very much at all. Early on, I was very much results driven. I knew these things were important, but I approached them as a box-ticking exercise instead of fully embracing them. I would give someone my five minutes of listening and check that box.

Checking the box is better than not even knowing that box is there to be checked, but being a good leader is about far more than simply checking a box. Internalizing these things is what gives leaders and teams resiliency and sustainability, which is why objectivity, listening and sensitivity to others are so important.

CHAPTER 6: TEAM BUILDING

"Communication underpins everything on your teams, but it also underpins the success of a business."

Whether you're building teams for the short or long duration, it's something you really have to get right. If you're on a really good team, everybody knows it and you can feel it. Similarly, if you're part of a not-so-good team, everybody knows it too. There are entire volumes written on teams and team building and what's contained in this book is far from exhaustive. What I'm going to cover in this chapter are a few guiding principles to help you as you get used to building and working with teams.

Without those principles and best practices, teams can form in a haphazard way. As you move further along your leadership journey, it's important to be deliberate in how you build teams. This will help ensure the team functions well and will also save a lot of wasted time and energy.

The first of the principles I'd like to introduce you to is chartering.

Team chartering

Team chartering is setting out a written framework for how your team functions. This is actually the start of the team-building process, because everyone works together to build the charter. Charters can be formal or informal, depending on the lifespan of the team. If you're in a team that will be together in the long term, your charter may be a document that you'll look at periodically, such as every year. If you're putting together an ad hoc team, your charter may look completely different. Whatever kind of charter you're creating, it's the process and functions that you need to go through that are important.

How to create a team charter

The first step towards creating a team charter, whether it's for a long– or short– duration team, is everybody on that team knowing its purpose. That might sound like I'm stating the obvious, but when you want to create alignment with people, sometimes stating the obvious is very important.

Sometimes that purpose might be established by those higher up in the organization and it might be a very general purpose, but as the team talks about what they're there for, it can become very specific. I believe this is an important part of starting to build a team and bring people together. Their first deliverable as a team is to create this charter, which sets out their purpose and gives them guidelines for how they work together.

This includes how the team is going to communicate with each other, such as email, video, telephone or face-to-face. At this stage, you can make sure that everybody is comfortable with the type of communication you're going to use. It's helpful for everybody to talk openly about how they're going to communicate and this also means you can discuss resolving conflict and how you are going to handle that within the team too.

You also set out how the team makes decisions. Is it a consensus-type decision? Is there a formal vote? Do you all talk about things together and give everyone a chance to share their input, but the team leader decides? You can really dig into your decision-making processes.

Part of creating your team charter also involves setting out norms and expectations for team members. One of the easy examples here is being on time for your meetings. Another that you have to consider, especially nowadays given that we all work digitally, is multitasking and specifically what level of multitasking is acceptable during a meeting.

For example, most of our resources are stored on the cloud and there are apps that you can use to take notes. When you're in a meeting and can see that someone is looking at their screen, you want to know that they haven't gotten lost on something that's not related to the discussions. Setting out these expectations and guidelines means that, instead of wondering whether someone is actually paying attention, you can take it as a given that they'll only be looking at their screen if it relates to what you're talking about.

In our company, we discovered how important it was to lay out some structure and framework for our teams about 10 years ago. In my experience, the higher-performing teams, in terms of the ones that perform well together, have gotten to this idea of team chartering either deliberately or accidentally.

When a team knows its purpose and has clear rules of engagement, and everybody honors those and moves forward with them, the team is able to work much more effectively.

The final element of chartering relates to the expectation of how long a team will last. When you put your team together, you want everybody to have a sense of how long it will last. This will enable you to decommission that team and recognize their work when they have completed it. You don't want the team to just quietly die. You want to have a deliberate dissolution of the team, and almost make it an event, so there's a deliberate beginning and a deliberate ending to the people on your team coming together.

Overcoming resistance to the concept of team charters

When you're introducing the concept of team charters, you might encounter some resistance. Whenever you do anything that's a change, there is likely to be some form of resistance, depending on the culture of the people around you and their experience within teams.

Leading people through change is part of your job as a leader. So, putting a team together, creating a charter and having those discussions is, in itself, a learning process in how to build and lead teams. It's a great opportunity! Once people have been through this process and worked within a team that has a charter, they become supportive of the process and would feel as though something was missing if this didn't happen when a new team came together.

It's never too late to go through this process, though. If you have a team that isn't working well together, it can definitely be recovered. To do that requires you, as leader, to show your vulnerability. When there is dysfunction in a team, everybody knows it and no one wants to talk about it, so having the courage to step up and state the obvious is the first step in this process.

Returning to your charter

When you have a long-standing team, such as an executive staff team for a company, members are going to come on and off that team. People and situations change over time. In the executive staff team at my organization, at times, we have found ourselves in the position where we don't feel as though our meetings are going right. It feels as though there's grit in the gears and things don't seem to be flowing.

A lot of the time, that's a sign that it's time to revisit your charter. When you look at it again, you might realize that you don't do this anymore, or that the situation has changed and certain elements aren't working anymore. This is a cue to figure out a new way of approaching things.

This is particularly evident at the time of writing with the Covid-19 pandemic and the big change in the way we interact socially that has come with it. I think the teams that are working well together at this time have been able to take this process and jumpstart it to look at the team in the context of where everybody is currently. The teams that have done this will be functioning much better than the teams that are simply wondering why things don't work any more.

Mike's leadership lesson: Lightbulb moment

One of my biggest lightbulb moments in relation to team building came when I was doing my MBA, which was the Ken Blanchard Executive MBA program.

Ken Blanchard is a world-famous author and his first big impact in the business world was a book called *One Minute Manager*. In his MBA program, he shares his model for high-performing teams. I was completing this MBA program when I was CEO, and one of the great things about my experience in that program was that I was developing my leadership and bringing my learnings back to work – which meant that my executive staff were pretty much going through the program with me.

As I was learning, and implementing what I had learned, I'd talk to my executive staff about what we were doing and what was coming next. At first, we would chat and laugh about it, but as time went on we were implementing things that made the company and the team better.

The idea of a team charter came from this MBA and it was a totally new concept for the company and the people working there. We started with it at the executive staff level. I wouldn't say we were a high-functioning team back then.

There were lots of internal conflicts within the team. We had many of the typical components of dysfunction within a team, in that we had lots of silos where people were just concerned with their own little world. We had overt conflict between team members, where the conflict was face-to-face, and we had behind-the-scenes conflict. The style in which the team was run meant that not everybody felt able to contribute to conversations, which had the effect of some team members feeling like they were on the sidelines, even though they weren't.

Unfortunately, we had pretty much all of those elements happening in our senior team, but as we learned how to build a high-performing team following the Ken Blanchard model, the executive staff began to come together and were much more cohesive and focused. We still had conflict, but it was managed in a constructive way.

Leadership lessons...

Conflict within teams is actually good, because you want to have those differing opinions within your team and you want people who are passionate about their ideas. However, if you don't have structure and an accepted way for that conflict to manifest, be discussed and to be resolved, it can cause issues.

In this scenario, conflict creates hurt feelings within your team. It can create animosity. One of the most important things that a team charter does is put all this on the table and allows everyone to have a dispassionate conversation about things that people feel very passionate.

Once you reach a resolution, your team begins to function much better than it did before. That's especially true in the case of executive staff or leadership teams. If those high-level teams are in conflict, everybody knows it, not only the people in the team but also those around them.

This comes back to the concept of understanding your wake that I talked about in the last chapter. You have a team wake as well as a personal one, and if your team isn't functioning properly, it will leave a big wake behind it that will impact even more people within your organization.

The benefit of being deliberate in team building, introducing a chartering process and bringing people within teams together with an openness to discuss issues is that you reduce this negative, disruptive wake. The sooner you can bring these conflicts and issues out into the open and get people talking about them, the sooner that team will shift to becoming a high-performing team.

Self-awareness: Being able to see how your way of working and the decisions you're making are affecting others is crucial for strong leaders, and strong leadership teams.

Openness

Openness in this context is people being willing to talk about what's going on within their team and how things are functioning.

I don't think there can ever be too much openness when it comes to how a team is functioning, how the members of the team relate to each other and what is impacting the team. The only time that openness could maybe become an issue is in the sense of off-topic oversharing, where people share things that have nothing to do with the team.

When this happens, it's important to take things 'offline'. We've actually found that the team chartering process really helps with this, because it allows you as the leader to step in and do just that.

It might be that the team is having a dialogue and an issue comes up that's impacting the team, but after talking about it for a few minutes it becomes quite obvious that the issue isn't really a team issue. It might be that one or two people have a few things they need to straighten out. Within your team chartering process you can identify a way that's acceptable to take these issues 'offline'.

What I mean by taking things 'offline' is that, if you're having a team meeting and two people are having a conversation within that meeting to the point that the rest of the team become bystanders to the discussion, anyone in the team can just say, 'Hey, can you guys take this offline?' It's a way to pause the discussion, and allow those two people to continue their conversation outside the meeting. They can then bring anything that's relevant to the wider team to the next meeting.

Openness is important in enabling this to happen. We all have to understand that sometimes there can be dialogue that's not relevant for the entire team. In this instance, there needs to be a mechanism to pull that dialogue out of the team environment and let people deal with whatever situations or challenges they're facing without impacting the rest of the team.

Communication

Communication is one of the most important aspects to focus on as a leader.

We have been running employee-opinion surveys at our company for about 15 years now. We have around 100 questions in the survey and we typically see about 95% of our employees complete the survey every year. The survey talks about leadership, communication, people's alignment with the company's strategy and their understanding of what's going on – it's a very comprehensive survey. When you look back at the surveys year after year, and you look at the various challenges that manifest in different areas of the company, they always come back to communication.

"A leader has to face reality. You can't fix a problem that you don't know you have."

I don't believe that there's a solution to a problem that can't be enhanced by communication. At the same time, it doesn't matter how good something is, if you don't have good communication you run the risk of something good turning out badly.

Communication underpins everything on your teams, but it also underpins the success of a business. An organization is a series of teams that are working together, which makes communication in relation to teams particularly important.

Essentially, communication is two things: it's conveying information, but it's also being willing to hear and absorb information.

I've already touched on the importance of discussing the different channels of communication that your team will use. There might be different types of communication that work in different scenarios. For example, email might be the preferred method of communication to get information sent out; but if you have a problem or challenge and need to brainstorm, in our organization that's always been a call for a face-to-face meeting.

Obviously, in recent times that's changed and we've all adapted to using online tools such as Zoom and Teams to have those more intense problem-solving or brainstorming sessions.

These concepts of how you communicate within your team and which mode of communication you use for different purposes is really just the first layer of communication you have to consider.

Post-meeting, you also need to think about how one team communicates with other teams within the company to explain what they've done and where things are. It's not only communication within the team that needs to be deliberate, but also communication outside of the team.

There has to be a deliberate process for communicating outside of your team. For example, after a meeting, we always check in by answering the following questions:

- What do we need to communicate to our stakeholders about this meeting?

- How are we going to communicate that?

- When is this communication going to come out?

It's important to understand that every team has an impact externally, whether that's on other teams within an organization or on external stakeholders. For teams to function well, and for organizations (which are a collection of teams working together) to function well, there needs to be agreement about what is being communicated by teams, who that's being communicated to, and how that process will work.

 # Mike's leadership lesson: Covid miscommunication

From time to time, miscommunication can happen within any organization and I'd like to share a story about how to deal with that as a leader, whether it was your miscommunication or someone else's.

At our company, I like to do periodic updates to the team. Especially during the last six months (at the time of writing in 2020-21), these updates have been every two to three weeks. I've put out formal video communications to help people deal with and manage their own anxiety as it relates to the Covid-19 situation.

Before I do these videos, I talk to my executive staff and we agree on the high points that I need to update the team. I then go away and turn that into a dialogue with the team that we hold over Zoom. When I've done the video meeting, a recording is sent out to everyone, so if they couldn't make the meeting they can watch it and anyone who was there has the recording to refer back to if they want.

As well as sending out the recording, we also follow up with a newsflash, which is a short written email to everyone in the company that provides a quick synopsis of what was said.

Not long ago, we were communicating a procedure that we needed to implement pretty quickly as it related to Covid personal protection. In the meeting, I told everybody that the procedure was, if you're going to be at your desk, don't wear a mask. If you're going to be away from your desk and walking around the building, wear a mask. If you're going to be in a meeting where you can't socially distance, wear a mask.

When the summary email of the meeting was sent out, it said: *CEO Mike Easley strongly suggests wearing masks.*

I saw that and thought, that's not what I said. It wasn't a suggestion. My first reaction was to want to find out what had happened. Often, when something like this happens, our first reaction is to pick up the phone or send an email in frustration to the person who got the communication wrong.

But that wasn't what I did. Instead, I called the VP of that division and said, "Hey, did you see the newsflash that came out summarizing the meeting about the use of masks?" They said, "Yes". So I asked, "Could you look at that again and make sure my message was right on that?" The VP looked at the communication again, realized that wasn't what was said in the meeting and a correction was sent out within half an hour.

This isn't the end of the story though. We all know that people tend to take information and hear what they want to hear. A lot of times, corrections don't sink in or people simply miss them.

I gave another video update about mask procedure. What I didn't do was say, "In case you didn't hear me last time, this is what I said..." Instead, I said, "I've been thinking about this a long time and I think I could just be a little more clear about what I meant. I've learned some things and I've thought about it..." And then I said the same thing that I said two weeks before, but in a way that didn't threaten people.

Leadership lessons...

Instead of rushing out and yelling at somebody who made a mistake, I took a step back and approached it from a wider perspective. I asked the question, "I'm curious to know, did I get this right? Could you look at this for me and give me a sanity check on what we're saying here?"

Rather than throwing stones at someone or laying blame, I corrected the miscommunication gently. This isn't only for the benefit of the person who sent the original miscommunication. Some people may have been thinking differently about the situation, or they may have read the first article but not seen the correction. I don't want to throw all of those people under a bus.

When there is miscommunication, I think leaders do well to not cast stones at the people who miscommunicated.

As leaders, we always have to take the extra time to not lay blame on people, to accept responsibility and then come to it again to try and fix it without throwing people under the bus.

You have to be confident in your leadership style to be able to do that, even though the situation may or may not be your fault. Blaming somebody for a mistake that was made and then setting yourself up as the savior of the day isn't what leadership is. The person who made the mistake knows it and they feel it.

If, as a leader, you can accept responsibility and not cast it on somebody else, that person remembers that, which builds loyalty and encourages them to do even better next time. Personally, I think that works well for organizations. I can certainly say that it works well in ours.

Empathy: By thinking about how someone else will feel when they have made a mistake, you can approach the situation from a place of empathy where not only do you correct the mistake, but everyone feels good about the outcome.

CHAPTER 7: SHAPING A TEAM

"As you're growing and developing your team, you're also growing and developing yourself."

As you move further along your leadership journey, and especially as you reach executive level, you should always be trying to grow and develop your team. Leading is an evolutionary process. As you're growing and developing your team, you're also growing and developing yourself. If you're ever satisfied that you're the leader that you want to be, you're probably not the leader you should be.

"Leaders need to develop a keen sense of empathy for those they lead."

One of the really critical aspects of being a leader is knowing when somebody within your team needs to find another team to be on. It's so easy to hide from the conflict that the team goes through when somebody needs to go.

In this situation, everybody on the team knows it, but rarely is anyone talking about it. It's the proverbial "elephant in the room" that everyone tiptoes around. As a leader, you can't avoid this conflict forever.

Mike's leadership lesson: Getting the CEO job

The first time I experienced this situation was when I joined PRECorp 20 years ago. This was my first CEO position and the environment I came into was one of extreme dysfunction. The acting CEO had put in for the job and didn't get it. He was the manager of engineering and operations, and in his time as acting CEO he had essentially restructured the company assuming that he would get the job.

He had built the team around him and when I came in as CEO, he was not happy at all. But the issues went beyond just this one person. The whole mentality of the team was one where people weren't used to making decisions for themselves. They were used to being told what to do.

The whole hierarchy of the company was built around what I'd describe as a "command and control" model, which meant that everybody was only as good as the person who was in front of them.

When I came on board, I had a guy who was mad about not getting the job and a company operating on a structure that I considered to be dysfunctional. It was a challenging environment to come into, especially as someone who had never been a CEO before.

When you first come into a team, you have to build trust and develop relationships. But imagine coming in as the leader of a team where, by organization, everybody is looking at you, wondering who you are, what you're about, and expecting that level of guidance.

Not only are you learning your new job and learning what issues need tackling, but you're also assessing the people that you have on your team and trying to figure out their competencies. Just one of those things is enough to do. Trying to juggle all of them is a challenge.

I remember one of the first staff meetings I held, where everybody came in and expected me to tell them what to do. They explained a situation and asked me what they should do. I said, "Well, what do you think you should do?" They were like deer in the headlights because they weren't used to being allowed to think for themselves.

In that first year or two, I think I often came across as though I didn't know what I was doing, because I would ask people what they thought they should do instead of just telling them. But I was really trying to get them to be more comfortable thinking for themselves.

During this first year, it became apparent that the former acting CEO had to go. He was being disruptive and doing everything he could to make sure that we were not successful. It took about a year before he decided to move on.

Leadership lessons...

If the people on your team are always looking for you to tell them what to do and which way to go, then you've limited yourself to only being as good as the person who is leading, because you always have to look to that person for guidance.

When you have someone who just doesn't mix with the rest of the team, or who is being disruptive, you need to have the courage to move them out of that team, or even out of the organization. If you don't, it will only create conflict within your team, or in some cases your whole organization.

Ego and self-awareness: You don't always have to be the smartest person in the room. Letting go of that and making space for others to step up will help the development of your leaders and their teams.

Identifying the underlying root of conflict

We often think of conflict management in terms of managing people – egos, in some cases, different personality types and how people interact with each other; or in terms of managing emotions because everybody is human and every now and then people bring their emotions into the team or a meeting.

But I believe that, on an organizational level, at the heart of every conflict you will find resources. The majority of organizations have limited resources. At this level, you don't have all the resources you'd like to solve the issues you're facing. Resources can be people, money or time, and they span an entire organization.

At an executive level, a team is operating at its healthiest when people are stepping outside of their departmental needs and looking at the overall requirements of the organization and the impact that its resources have on consumers. This is when you can start to have authentic and healthy conversations about resources.

For example, at PRECorp, our sales are going down because of some declines in the energy industry. Our expenses are naturally going up and we can't automatically increase the price of our product to make up for falling sales volumes and rising expenses. When this happens, people and teams start to compete for resources within the organization. This is the kind of conflict that a leader needs to be aware of.

If you don't recognize that source of conflict, and bring people together to remind them of the mission and vision that your organization has, even the best people will start to lose sight of that. This is when the fabric of your team starts to get damaged and that can manifest itself as bickering between departments or teams. But the underlying cause of these conflicts is resources.

This is an issue we're facing at PRECorp as I write this book. We've been cutting costs and carrying out cost containment for a long time and we've done a pretty good job of reducing expenses, but now we're getting to the stage where trimming more areas really hurts.

When you're in a situation like that, it's really important to remind the team of the bigger picture. You have to come back to the bigger purpose behind your organization, because if your teams don't have awareness of that bigger purpose it starts to get really tough when they are competing for resources.

As I said, most people won't recognize that the conflicts stem from this competition for resources. But, as a leader, being aware of the underlying reason for conflict within a team, or between teams, is one of the most important elements to help you successfully manage conflict. You need to dig deeper and look beyond what's obvious, to find the root cause of the conflict; and resource conflicts are one of the biggest underlying issues, in my experience.

How to manage resource conflicts

At PRECorp, we're communicating the bigger issues that we're facing with everyone in the organization. We're being open about our declining sales and our ongoing efforts to reduce expenses. We're also leveraging accelerating technologies to reduce our costs and digitizing processes as much as possible. As the leader of that organization, I have to communicate the landscape that we're in with all of our employees.

The executive team includes the ones who really need to take a deep dive into the gory details of what we're doing to survive in that landscape. The executive staff needs to be aware of the major conflicts and landscape in which they're working. This awareness helps prevent the resource allocation issues from manifesting as bickering between departments or teams, or even within the executive team itself.

It's the executive team's job to create a plan to deal with these underlying sources of conflict and to find a clear path through. There will definitely be trade-offs. Some departments, or functions within departments, might change or completely go away. Sacrifices have to be made, but the trick to doing this successfully and constructively is for the executive staff to have a really solid understanding of the conflict that they're trying to solve.

At this stage, it evolves into a negotiation within the executive team to determine how to use the resources your organization has to meet its purpose as closely as you can, without your members suffering too much.

Once you have created a plan that the executive team signs off on, the question then becomes how you can deliver that to the team, and facilitate the results of your decision making.

This is where real leadership comes in, because it can be so easy for the person who's offering up resources from their part of the company to help a different area altogether, to assume a victim mentality, or to blame others within the business if they are losing resources.

True leaders make sure that everyone is reminded of the organization's overall purpose, so once a decision like this is made, the executive team is communicating it to their teams, and so on. This helps teams who are making sacrifices understand that it's for the greater good, and shows them that they're contributing to the overall mission of the business.

This approach also means that teams who are the beneficiaries of resources taken from elsewhere understand that these resources come with a sacrifice. Hopefully, what happens is that these teams go away with an appreciation for what's been done and, therefore, are more diligent with the resources they've been given; and are more focused on delivering the expected return for the organization and its members.

Reframing changes and resource allocation in this way means that people across your organization are more likely to support them. They see those resources as a gift and, therefore, try to do well with that gift. I believe this is the kind of leadership that you get out of a really high-functioning team that's able to dip below the apparent conflicts to get to the heart of their causes, which are often resource related.

Being able to come up with a plan that keeps the company's purpose as the ultimate objective is the next step. From here, it's about delivering those results in such a way that all of your team members feel empowered by the direction that the company is going and the changes that are being made, rather than feeling victimized.

Mike's leadership lesson: Business resources

As I said earlier, at PRECorp, we're more resource-constrained than we ever have been. Covid-19 has played a part in that; but in our case, it's more to do with how the energy industry is changing.

I explained the concept that I've just unpacked with my executive team. I held a meeting and I told them that I wanted to talk about what we were heading into. I said that I knew things had been getting tighter, that we had been cutting expenses to become more efficient, and that we were continually looking at ways to do more with fewer resources. I also told them that we were reaching the point where we'd be cutting to the bone, in some areas.

"I'm concerned that, as a result, we're going to see conflict come up that nobody's prepared to deal with," I said.

Then I talked about this concept of competition for resources between business departments and I pointed out that, within the world in general, competition for resources underlies many conflicts.

"What's going to happen is that all the areas of conflict that we've had before, that we think we've resolved, are going to rear their ugly heads again, and it's going to feel as though that's the conflict. But, in actual fact, we have this resource conflict underpinning them," I explained.

After this conversation with my team, I shared this narrative with the entire company, although I framed it slightly differently and talked about how we might be experiencing more conflict, but also that the reason for this conflict is potentially deeper than we realize. I asked everyone to think about that and, when they experience any conflict, to remember their mission and to look at the bigger picture.

Fast forward a few days, I was having one-to-ones with my executive team. People were coming to me very concerned and the conversations started with, "Were you talking about me? In that conversation were you trying to send me a message? Were you trying to tell me that I need to be a team player? Did somebody tell you that I wasn't a team player? Because here are all the reasons why I am a team player..."

They each reeled off a huge list of things that they were feeling anxiety over in relation to everybody else. They all took this conversation very personally, as though I had been talking about them doing something that wasn't right.

In response I said, "This wasn't something that I was telling the team that we're doing. My whole purpose was to equip you to understand that we may be feeling more anxiety about certain things (that feel like normal things to feel anxiety about) but that, in actual fact, are a sign of an underlying issue. Maybe you're feeling some anxiety, like I was talking about..."

At this point, the conversation became totally different. "So you weren't talking about me?" "No." "You were talking about how I might be feeling anxiety and concern that I maybe haven't felt recently?" "Yes."

This realization was followed by a long, uncomfortable silence where I could see each person self-reflect and think, "Oh man, I'm *feeling* things."

Leadership lessons...

Conflict in business or work is like any emotional conflict that we encounter. Or, any problem that we fear. If you can name it, you can fix it.

When you're leading a team and you're managing conflict, it's important to help people name what they're feeling. You don't even have to get it exactly right, but if you can name it in a way that allows people to look at it, talk about it, feel it and deal with it, you can find a resolution.

This then moves into the process of negotiation, where you talk about the various trade-offs that may resolve the conflict. I think in a proper resolution to a conflict, everybody moves a little. Nobody gets exactly what they want, there is always give and take. But it's the ability to name the issue and step back from it that allows you to stop feeling it and start talking about it. This will lead you to the point of negotiating, brainstorming and problem solving to figure out what you can do to move forward.

It's incumbent on the leader to make sure you're guiding your team through this. To do that, you have to step outside of yourself and see it from an observer's perspective. You can't be in there with them, but you are there to guide people as they reflect on their emotions, experience the conflict and finally get ready to negotiate and resolve it.

Empathy: As a leader, you need to see conflicts from all perspectives to enable you to help everyone navigate those in a healthy and constructive way.

Keep your eye on the purpose

Most companies will have a stated purpose or mission, and some teams may also have a stated purpose. If you're the leader of a team, or the leader of many teams, it's your job to know yourself and communicate what that purpose is with your people.

You have to keep your eye on the purpose. It can help if you can connect that team or organizational purpose to a worthwhile cause that is bigger than the self, because that helps people to step out of themselves and focus on that broader purpose.

Hopefully, you, or the leaders before you, have already established what that bigger purpose is. As you resolve conflict, it's important to keep everybody focused on that bigger purpose; and on the reason for them being there and for giving their time and energy to that purpose.

Self-awareness is key for encouraging self-awareness in others

If you want to move from being a good leader to being a great leader, you have to be aware of what's going on inside yourself.

You have to follow your feelings, which can be a scary thought, especially if you're an engineer like me. I would say I spent two-thirds of my career thinking that feelings were an impediment. I believed that if you felt a certain way about something you had to block those feelings in order to make decisions. I was lucky enough to get through those first two-thirds of my career without doing too much damage to myself or the others around me despite having this belief.

This concept of having self-awareness ties back into the continuum we're talking about in this book, of moving from self-leadership, to leading others, to leading organizations. As I said in the first part of the book, the way you lead yourself is to pay attention to what's going on inside you, you become aware of it and you think about it.

Going back to the example I gave in my leadership lesson, where my managers were coming to me with all of this anxiety – I remember one in particular who was giving me passionate justification for why he was a team player and part of me wanted to jump in and engage with him there.

But because of my ability to take a step back and view the situation from an outside perspective, I was able to think about what I was feeling and why I was feeling that way. In my experience, often when you're talking to somebody and you begin to feel anxious, or angry, or you're feeling emotional energy building up, there's a good chance that it's *their* emotional energy coming at you.

At this point, you have two choices: you can enter the game and feed that back to them, in which case it often escalates, or you can recognize the emotion, and the fact that it's developed during this conversation. This allows you to see that it's the other person who is feeling anxious and that enables you to step back and make a conscious decision about how to move the conversation forward rather than allowing it to be hijacked by that emotional energy.

Self-leadership is deciding to take that different tack and, as a leader, you model that for the people around you. It's this continuum of being able to do that for yourself, and in doing so you're then able to do that with and for others.

Sometimes, you might decide that you need to engage emotionally with someone, rather than take the calm approach. If you do that, you have to make sure you're intentionally engaging emotionally and not being reactive, though. The less you can react and the more you can do things with intention, the better.

If you're not paying attention to that energy, that's when you can get into trouble; because it becomes a back and forth and the energy escalates. Your aim should be to de-escalate that energy and bring it down to a manageable level, because when emotions get high, we lose our ability to think rationally.

Coping with an uneven power differential

There may be situations where you're on the wrong side of an uneven power differential, or where you're facing a group of people who are ramped up with this energy. My advice in this situation is not to panic and to let it wash over you.

It's a lot like being in the ocean with waves crashing over you. You know what's coming, you brace for it and the waves crash around you. All of a sudden, a really big wave comes with a lot of energy and you fight it as it crashes over you. The next thing you know, you're being pushed against the sand, there's a tumble of white water, you're getting rolled with the current and you feel lost, scared and, maybe even for a moment, as though your world is coming to an end. As the wave passes through, you break the surface, gasping for breath.

The other option in this scenario is not to fight the big wave that comes crashing down around you, but to flow with it and glide with it. As the wave passes through, it takes you with it; but you put your feet down and stand up, realizing that you're only in knee-deep water.

When you're in a meeting or interacting with someone where there's this uneven power differential, think about it as that wave that's going to crash over you. You can't stop it and you can't change it. If you fight it, it will take control and push you under, but if you flow with it and go with the energy of that wave, you'll end up in shallower water where you can stand and be in a much better position where you're ready to connect more rationally.

Staying calm and not panicking allows you to connect rationally with that group or that person, even if you have to wait for a few more waves to hit you before you find the right moment to connect in that way.

PART 3:

Managing & Leading/ Organization Focus

Managing and leading an organization is the next step on your leadership journey once you're effectively managing teams; just as effectively managing a team was the natural follow up to being able to lead yourself. This is simply the next stage in the continuum of your growth as a leader, which all started with self-management.

Every step along the way, you're dealing with increased complexity, and leading an organization is where your ability to live, work and deal with complexity becomes very important.

Complexity in this sense, especially as you're dealing with people, is really about how comfortable you are dealing with uncertainty and how easily you can take a step back to enable you to look at multiple ideas that might seem conflicting at times, with a view to finding a path forward that is the best choice for the organization. Leading an organization is essentially managing several different teams and your role is to engage all of these teams to move towards the organization's goals.

The more effective you are as a leader at creating a vision that everybody understands and can buy into, the more successful you'll be at engaging teams and leveraging them to accomplish what needs to be done.

Underpinning your ability to manage multiple teams, manage an organization and move the people within that organization towards a common goal, there needs to be an understanding of what organizations are and how they work.

As someone who is leading an organization, you have to be able to think and look ahead, at least as far as anyone within your teams and, ideally, farther than them.

It can help to think of it in terms of a car's headlights. As the leader, your view is like the headlights on a car at night and you need to cast that view further than anyone else who works in the organization. If you can't do that then you're likely to encounter conflict.

Vision really is this ability to think in complex terms, operate in areas of the unknown and consider a whole range of factors to make assumptions that, more often than not, are correct. As you begin to lead organizations, having an awareness of what vision looks like and where your vision lines up with the teams you're leading is very important. Where your vision doesn't match or exceeds the teams you're leading, you'll struggle to find success.

Your ability to engage and leverage teams really depends on you having that vision and being able to imagine further into the future than anyone else.

The further along the leadership continuum you move, the more important it is to be self-aware. Understanding what's driving you and why you're making certain decisions is extremely important as you lead other people and lead an organization.

The No-Os of Leadership

A large part of leadership involves making decisions. There are some decisions that you can make fast and others that you can make more slowly. When you first start leading organizations, you will most likely have a really rigorous process for making decisions and spend a lot of time thinking about them. You'll get into the consequences of those decisions, not only in terms of how they impact your immediate team, but also the teams that they lead and the people within those teams.

As you gain experience, decision making becomes easier. Humans are best at recognizing patterns and the more decisions you make, the more likely you are to come across patterns that you've seen before, which will eventually mean you might not need to carry out that detailed level of analysis every time.

Experienced leaders who have been successful at leading teams and organizations have developed a vast portfolio of pattern recognition to help them know what to do. But even when you have this experience, there's a test that you should always be aware of and that's the three things you should always bear in mind as you're making decisions. I call them the 'No-Os of Leadership'.

If a leader pays attention to these No-Os and checks their decision against each of these three factors, I think it helps them to make decisions that work better for them and for their organization. As a reminder, the three No-Os are ego, libido and dinero.

 Ego – If a leader makes a decision out of ego, that decision will typically put the leader at the center of it. An ego-based decision isn't looking out for or serving the organization, and is all about the leader, which doesn't work well. True leadership is a desire to serve, not to be served.

 Libido – This can be thought of as decisions to engage in inappropriate relationships in the workplace. But if you scale it up, libido is about a leader using their power inappropriately, often to disempower others. Checking your decisions against libido is about making sure there isn't an attraction to something or someone that's driving your decision.

 Dinero – A decision driven by dinero is one that's serving the leader financially. The important question here is, "Is there a financial or other reward to me personally by making this decision that is hidden and not a normal part of performance compensation?" Again, any decision made based on dinero usually doesn't work well for the organization or the team.

Ultimately, if you look at some of the epic leadership failures out there, you can see that this trifecta of ego, libido and dinero have gone awry in the decision-making process. We'll talk more about these concepts in Chapter 11, and you'll have noticed some of the stories I've already shared have included No-Os leadership failures.

We're going to start, however, by looking more closely at engaging teams across an organization and leveraging your teams to get the best outcomes.

CHAPTER 8: ENGAGING TEAMS

"Engaged employees translate to engaged teams and that translates to an effective organization."

Engaging teams in this context centers around how you develop and unify multiple teams to work towards a common goal. As someone who is leading multiple teams, your aim is to figure out how to get them to work together in the most effective way for your organization.

To scale this up to an organizational level, you need a solid understanding of teamwork. You need to plan and organize around developing teamwork and engaging your teams; and in doing so, you'll ultimately be pursuing excellence through the efforts that your teams are making, as well as delivering on the overall mission or purpose of the organization.

Developing teamwork

Developing teamwork is very important for anyone who is good at managing and leading, and who is focused on the needs of the overall organization. But, developing teamwork is actually very counterintuitive and the mistake you could make is thinking that you're going to be the one who is developing teamwork, getting in there, moving pieces around and pulling levers; and that couldn't be farther from the truth.

People who are able to lead organizations don't develop teamwork by telling everybody what to do. They develop teamwork by creating systems and ways of thinking about problem solving and how people relate to each other. As a leader at this organizational level, you have to create a culture that allows people to work independently from your day-to-day input.

By the time you're leading an organization, you've followed and understood the ideas and concepts in the first two parts of this book. At this point, you have team leaders who are very competent and self-aware, and who are doing a good job with their teams. Your job, as the leader of the organization, is to bring all of that together and stand back. That's the end game. If you do such a good job of developing your people and your teams that this is the result, you bounce between feeling really proud that they can function without you and really scared that they can function without you. It's a double-edged sword.

If you look at an organization that's highly successful, functioning well and highly adaptive, and you peel back the layers, you get down to the people within that organization. What you find when you reach the people is that they each have a clear understanding of the organization's overall vision, as well as their role and contribution towards it.

What I've discovered is that what makes an organization successful is all the individuals within the organization knowing how they can contribute personally to its success. That is the first step in developing teamwork, everyone knowing what the big-picture goal is and how they are contributing to that.

"Leaders Worth Following are willing to teach."

Once you have that individual level of understanding, you bring them together in teams and help them understand how they contribute to their team, as well as how their team interacts with other teams to accomplish that vision. This is why having a clear, compelling vision is so important. Again, this comes back to the concept of having a noble cause involved, which can help people engage individually, which in turn brings teams together.

The other thing that's very important in developing teamwork is that the culture of your company invites feedback from your employees and teams. I'm not just talking about asking for feedback, but also making sure that you do something with that feedback.

Companies that are highly successful have a deliberate and dependable process for gathering feedback from their entire team and using that feedback to eliminate friction within the organization; and to make the organization a better place for everybody.

The feedback system you introduce needs to make people feel comfortable expressing their opinions, and the results of the feedback need to be open and transparent.

A company that collects employee feedback but doesn't share it, or what they're doing with it, isn't going to be successful. What you have to do is show your employees, year after year, what feedback you received, what you did with it, and how that has contributed to the overall success of the company. Taking action on that feedback is important.

Doing that regularly and consistently will help create a sense of teamwork, not only in the sense that everybody is on the same team from the bigger perspective, but also that there's a sense of alignment among people on separate teams and the understanding that their thoughts and opinions make a difference to the organization. This creates buy-in and engaged employees. Engaged employees translate to engaged teams and that translates to an effective organization.

The final area to focus on in terms of developing teamwork is demonstrating a commitment to your employees by providing training and development for people. One of the strongest ways to develop teamwork, and to develop people in the process, is by providing opportunities for people to work cross-functionally.

Teamwork is everybody on a team working together in the same direction, but you can scale that across an organization by focusing on this concept of cross-functional working and training.

When different teams and different people from across the organization have an opportunity to work together, it creates a real sense of camaraderie. Similarly, giving people the chance to be part of a cross-functional training and development program accelerates that feeling of teamwork across a company and the silos within that company are reduced.

At this stage, people relate not only to others within their team, but also cross-functionally within the organization; and this is when an organization itself feels like a team rather than a disparate bunch of teams who are working loosely together.

Having a compelling vision, and each individual understanding their role in accomplishing that vision; giving individuals the opportunity to provide feedback and knowing that their opinions matter; and providing cross-functional developmental opportunities are the best ways to develop teamwork in the sense that your entire organization is a team.

Aligning external teams with your company vision

This idea of everyone being aligned with your overall company vision extends to any external contractors, partners or teams that you might be working with. When you're leading at an organizational level and you form partnerships or relationships with key vendors or contributors outside of your organization, they need to understand your company's culture. There needs to be at least some alignment in culture, and if your culture doesn't align with that of a vendor or contractor, you're inviting friction into your organization.

As you look to develop relationships outside of your organization to help you accomplish your vision, it really helps for you to share your vision so they understand what you're about and why it is that you do what you do. There doesn't need to be perfect alignment between you, but those external vendors, entities and partners need to understand their roles and how they fit into your culture in order for you to work well together.

Planning and organizing

Imagine that your organization is an Olympic athlete who is constantly training and constantly improving. You start to make minor shifts to the way you hold your body, or maybe move your hand, in order to improve your performance.

The organizational version of this is that everyone brings their own set of skills, passions, strengths and weaknesses to the organization. Many times, a person's position might not actually play to what they're really passionate about or particularly good at. This is where you, as the leader, have to be planning and organizing to make sure that you have the right people in the right seats on the bus.

An issue that you can often encounter within companies is that there might be a person performing a particular job that they're not especially good at, or where they struggle with certain aspects of a job. Often our temptation as a leader is to think, "That person isn't cutting it, we need to get somebody else to do that job."

However, we need to step back from that approach and instead take the time to really understand that person and maybe see that they have a skillset that isn't quite right for either where that position is or where it's evolved to, but that could be better utilized in another job. You have to think about whether there are other places in your organization where that person's contribution can be fully felt and where you can harness their passion.

An important element of planning and organizing your company is having talent move intentionally around your organization. Consider the costs of onboarding someone and what you have to invest to not only train them in their task, but also in helping them to understand how they align to the vision of the company. You don't want to lose people to the outside because they feel a job has run its course or it's not meeting their passion.

In fact, encouraging people to understand their alignment to the company vision can even help them to self explore and question whether their skills and talents are really contributing to the company. As a leader you want to enable those frank conversations, not only from a performance perspective, but also from the perspective of personal development.

You ideally want to have those conversations way before you have performance issues, and you will find that it's much easier to approach people about this internal movement when you really understand what they're passionate about and where their strengths lie.

The aim is to plan for the development of your people and their personal growth, and to align that with the growth of the organization. Intentionally moving talent around your organization ensures that everybody is contributing their best self to the broader mission.

This is important for leaders to recognize – and it's particularly important for the person who's running an organization to recognize – because it makes much more sense to lose people to other positions within your organization than to lose them to outside of your organization.

In addition, when people see opportunities for growth within the organization and understand how they fit in, it gives even more of an opportunity to develop teamwork and commitment to the company.

Mentorship: developing talent and pursuing excellence

Over the years I spent learning from Ken Blanchard, he taught me we are the average of the eight people that we interact with and value the most, not only at work but in many areas of our lives. When you are looking for ways to help further develop the talent in your team to enable others to pursue excellence, mentoring is an obvious place to start.

You can have informal and formal mentors in your life, but what I'm talking about here is having a formal mentorship relationship. This means you're describing it as such and dedicating time to building that relationship. The words you use in relation to being a mentor, or a mentee, are important because words create intention and intention creates outcome. I believe you need to have that intention to get the most out of mentorship in a leadership context. We can all benefit from having mentors at any stage in our career, and we will also get positives from being a mentor for others.

If you are looking for a mentor to further your leadership journey, it's important to find someone who has the qualities and values that you are trying to seek. You're looking for someone whose character and values will rub off on you and make you better for the time you spend with them.

Depending on why you're looking for a mentor, you may also be seeking someone with a specific skill that you want to develop further, or someone with expertise or insight in an area that you are working on personally. The act of seeking out a mentor shows your commitment to your leadership journey and that you are seeking to improve.

Mike's leadership lesson: Do you do charity work?

At the time of 9/11, I'd been CEO at PRECorp for a little over a year. When it happened, I remember feeling a call to leadership and service that manifested as "I've got to do better and up my game." Understandably, after the terrorist attack on U.S. soil there was a lot of fear in the country. At PRECorp, we decided to run an initiative called our "Celebration of Community Champions".

Super Bowl champions Kevin Holloway and William Perry got involved. We did a bus tour across our service territory, visiting our small communities, and we created a lot of positive energy by celebrating volunteers and their communities. This initiative resulted in me being invited to speak at an annual meeting of the National Electrical Cooperative Association. That's where I met Kevin Freiberg.

Kevin was a panel moderator at that meeting and, after his presentation, I did something bold. I approached him and asked, "Do you do any charity work?" He looked at me kind of funny and said, "What do you mean?" I replied, "Well, I work for a not-for-profit, as a CEO. We don't have a lot of money and I'm sure I can't afford you but, man, if you do any charity work I sure would appreciate your help." He laughed, told me to give him a call and follow up with him.

That conversation resulted in Kevin coaching me, helping me with strategic planning at PRECorp and has led to a really interesting relationship that I value to this day (you might have noticed that Kevin wrote the Foreword to this book).

Leadership lessons…

I was at the beginning of my journey as a cooperative CEO and I recognized I would benefit from support from someone with more experience. That awareness was what made me see how Kevin could support me as I developed and grew into my leadership role.

The important thing is that I didn't shrink away and hide from what I noticed. I found the courage to ask Kevin for his help. The worst that would have happened was that he said no, but by having the courage to approach him, I found an understanding and supportive mentor who has been part of my leadership journey for many years.

Self-awareness: You need to know where you need help to be able to identify the right people to mentor you at different stages in your leadership journey and, to do that, you need self-awareness.

As a leader within an organization, you may have an opportunity to mentor some of the people within your teams. This is part of giving back as a leader, because we all have a unique set of skills and abilities that make us special. Having the ability to share those with others puts you in a position to be a mentor.

When you become a mentor, you have to understand that part of your role is to hold up a mirror for your mentee to help them more clearly see their strengths, areas in which to improve and opportunities. As a mentor, you also have to understand how best to hold that mirror up for different people, so that you can provide each individual with feedback in a way that works for them.

Building rapport and trust is an important part of the mentor-mentee relationship. You have to be able to sit with your mentee without judgment and accept them where they are. You'll give them feedback, but you'll do it in a meaningful, tactful, and caring way. When you have this rapport and trust, both of you will take positives from your relationship.

Giving the people within your teams the opportunity to find and work with mentors in your organization is incredibly powerful and encourages everyone to pursue excellence in their own way. For me, being both a mentee and a mentor is an opportunity to get better at what you do. A large part of being a leader is having self-awareness, as

I've explained already; and embracing mentorship, whether you take the role of student or teacher, is an opportunity to get better at what you do and to grow as a person.

Why become a mentor and how to do it

Many of us are aware of the benefits of being a mentee and having a mentor, but there is a great deal to gain from becoming a mentor for others who are at a different stage of their leadership journey. The further along your journey you get, the more opportunities you will have to give back in this way.

Mentorship is all about building relationships, learning from each other, sharing, teaching and experiencing, all of which means you will benefit whichever side of the relationship you are on.

Around the time I was writing this book, a young man was appointed CEO at another cooperative and he moved into that role from one in senior management. I remember what it felt like when I first took the reins of leadership like that, how frightening it was at times, and how I definitely made some missteps. I phoned this guy and said, "Hey, I know this is all new, and I know what it feels like to be starting out on this journey. I think you're going to be great at it, but if there's anything I can do to help, or you think me sharing my experiences could help you get better faster, then I'd be more than willing to do that." We have been speaking every two weeks since I made this call.

I put myself out there and volunteered to be his mentor, not because I felt that he had any specific weaknesses, but because I've been on that journey and I know how valuable that support can be. I have also made a commitment to him, and to myself, that I'll be available for those calls every two weeks. It's really important to make that time commitment and to honor it, both for your mentee and for yourself.

However, these calls with this CEO haven't only been beneficial for him, they've helped me too. I'm learning from him and our conversations remind me of things that are still good to know, even after all of these years.

If you do want to volunteer to be someone's mentor, you have to approach the conversation with thought and empathy. If you see someone who is maybe struggling, or who you feel you could help, you have to make yourself available to help them without taking away their sense of power or, as it's often called, their sense of agency.

My advice, if you see someone struggling, is to first ask them for permission to give them feedback. The conversation might go a little something like this, "Hey, I've been watching you and I think you do a great job, but I noticed this one thing and I wondered if you'd be open to some feedback on this?" More often than not, that person will say "yes", and if they don't, then you know that they aren't open to this kind of relationship at this time.

The first few times you approach someone to offer support in this way, it might feel strange. You might question yourself and what makes you feel you're an expert in this area, but please, trust in your intentions being good and work through those feelings. We all have the voice of "I am not..." inside of us. It tells us things like, "I'm not good enough; I'm not smart enough; I'm not strong enough..." you get the idea. There can be times in our lives when that voice seems to be yelling at us. However, what we always have to do, both in our capacity as leaders and in our lives in general, is be aware of that voice and find a way to shut it down. It's common for this voice of "I am not..." to pop up when you're offering to teach someone something, but always remember that you have a set of unique skills and strengths, the combination of which isn't like anyone else.

If you find this voice of "I am not..." starting to shout when you either offer to mentor someone or are asked to support someone in this way, take a moment to remind yourself that you are good at what you do, you do have talent, you do have individuality and you can contribute in many different ways.

Remember too, that this relationship isn't only about you sharing your knowledge and experiences with someone else. It is an opportunity for you to learn, as well as to teach. You are pursuing excellence, just as the person you are supporting is.

There is a very powerful concept called "beginner's mind", which means that in some cases people who are new to something might approach it in a very different way. They don't have preconceptions about how something should be done, and no one has told them that something can't be done. When you share how you would approach a particular task or situation, be humble and allow the person you are talking to the space to build on your approach. The best way to get the most out of the mentor-mentee relationship is to view it as a learning experience for yourself, as well as an opportunity to help somebody else.

You are the only person who you have the power to change

It's very powerful to remember that you are the only person who you have the power to change. You can't change anybody else, and trying to is often frustrating. When you go into a relationship as a mentor, go into it with humility; and remember that you are there to support the other person, not to "fix" them.

I can tell you, from my years of experience, that trying to "fix" people doesn't work. I have certainly made the mistake of trying in my time, but this never achieves the outcome I'm looking for. What I have learned is that I can support people and I can help them see a possible future, but they have to build that future for themselves. You're holding space for that person and being supportive, rather than giving them instructions on what to do.

If someone comes to you with problems or challenges that they want to discuss, resist the urge to tell them what you would do and instead ask them, "What do you think you might want to do about that?" Give them a safe space where they can talk about their thoughts and find their own answers. It can be challenging, but you have to allow people to figure things out for themselves. People can fix and grow themselves, but this isn't a process that can be forced or one that you have the power to control.

Identifying your passion

If you are new to being a mentor and are unsure of where to begin, my advice is to think about what you're passionate about – both in and out of the workplace. What do you really enjoy doing? Do you lose track of time when you're working on a particular project, and suddenly realize that two hours have gone by in what feels like a flash? The answers to both of those questions are really good indicators of things that come naturally to you and that are your strengths.

When you're trying to identify what aspect of your work you're most passionate about, ask yourself that question about losing track of time. When you feel like this, you have entered a flow state, which, without going into too much of the science behind it, means that all the parts of your brain are fully engaged in working on that task or project. Identifying what causes you to enter a flow state is a good starting point for identifying the skills and areas where you might be able to offer others support to help them grow and learn.

Open communication enhances teamwork

Developing mentor-mentee relationships encourages open and honest communication, which is essential for fostering an environment that encourages strong teamwork. However, this is just one way in which to create open communication in a business.

There's no doubt that teamwork is really enhanced in a culture where there's open communication. It's important for people to have a line of sight from who they are and what they do, to the ultimate vision and purpose of the company. That's critical to get engagement.

It follows that, if you want people to be engaged in the organization to that level and to have that sense of teamwork, you need to communicate. Communication is the lubrication for that engagement and it's an essential piece of the puzzle because it feeds engagement and it feeds people.

"Leading with empathy will help you to empower, and if you can empower others; they will, in turn, embrace your leadership."

In this time of lockdowns and remote working, whether you've intentionally chosen to make your workforce remote or it's something you've done because of the pandemic, your communication has got to increase. Communication isn't just talking *at* people, it's talking *with* people and it's everybody's job. How leaders model communication, especially when people are under stress, is really critical to maintaining the sense of team and the sense of togetherness when people are working more remotely.

If supervisors understand this then they're going to be communicating more with their people. If you're leading an organization, you have to communicate with people in new and different ways. At PRECorp, for instance, we've become much more comfortable with video communications.

In 2020, I started doing a quick update to the whole team every two weeks. This is an all-company, online Zoom meeting where I communicate content and challenges to the team in a way that they've never seen before. I'm giving them an insight into the big picture, as well as some of the day-to-day challenges that we're facing as a company, and that I'm facing as a CEO. I think people feel more informed and committed as a result.

This bi-monthly dialogue has created a sense of teamwork and unity. When you think about it, people everywhere want to have a sense of belonging, and when they have that it creates resilience in them. Being honest and communicating regularly with everyone in my company is teamwork. We all like to belong to a team because it creates that sense of belonging that we, as humans, crave. That sense of belonging also feeds teamwork.

By being honest, authentic, and showing some vulnerability in my communications with my team, particularly around the challenges we're facing, I'm able to reassure them that we're all in it together and that, in turn, fosters that sense of belonging.

People are more accepting of video communications than they were before and I think this is a great opportunity for leaders to leverage their time. I used to have one, annual all-team meeting where we'd pull everyone in the company together physically and I'd tell them what was going on. If you asked people if they'd like me to go back to doing an annual meeting with all the pomp and ceremony, or to continue with the twice-weekly, 20-minute Zoom meetings, I think they'd much rather have these shorter, more frequent communications.

Mike's leadership lesson: Open-door policy

As CEO, I've always had an open-door policy where anyone could come and see me at any time and talk to me about anything.

Early on, I would have employees take advantage of my open-door policy. They'd come and talk to me about issues and I would feel like these were issues I had to fix. I would then try to reach down the organization to "fix" them, but I learned pretty quickly that's not the way to do it because that doesn't work well for anyone.

Of course, there might be instances where there's harassment going on, an injustice or policy violation that you have to get involved with, because you have a duty of care as a leader. But for the most part, I take this feedback as a datapoint and use that time to connect with the people in the organization, and to get a sense of where things are.

I thank people for their information, I let them feel valued for taking the time to speak to me and, in doing that, people feel valued and they feel heard.

There were sometimes opportunities for me to make a suggestion or ask a question that related to what the person talked to me about in a one-to-one, but I didn't directly intervene.

With the Covid-19 pandemic, things have obviously changed. I tried to take my open-door policy to the next level by having one-to-one Zoom meetings with all of my team members during 2020. My aim was to have spoken to every one of my employees, one-to-one, by the end of 2020; and I managed to speak to the majority of them on this level. I was having two or three calls each day. Sometimes these calls lasted five minutes, sometimes 25 minutes.

My first questions in these calls are, "How are you doing? How's it going for you? How is your family?" People have different family situations, with some people's families near and others far away. Some of them had pretty tough things happen in their families during this year, and I feel that it's my duty as CEO to check in with them to get a sense of how my team and, ultimately, the organization are doing.

Leadership lessons...

It's really important if you're adopting an open-door policy as a CEO that you manage this in the right way. In some organizations, this might be concerning for other managers who might worry about their teams having a direct pipeline to the CEO.

I believe it's really important for people leading teams, including CEOs, to be open to hearing what other people have to say. That being said, that doesn't mean that if you hear something you have to "fix" it or act on it.

If you develop the trust of your leadership team and your supervisors, they will know that the open-door policy you have as a CEO is valuable and that the outcomes from what you hear from people are informative not reactive. It's important that people don't feel like there has been a violation of the chain of command. You don't want your managers to feel threatened by you, as the CEO, connecting on that one-to-one level with your employees.

Having teams that are healthy enough, and having the ability as CEO to dive in and connect with your employees and have that dialogue in an environment where no-one thinks twice about it, is a pretty great goal and a worthy outcome.

As a leader, this allows me to gather data points on how the organization is doing, and it's a great opportunity to put my finger on the pulse of the organization and to know how my people are doing. Making that personal connection is pretty powerful stuff, and it's important to think about how, as leaders, we can continue to leverage that in the future.

Empathy: Meeting people where they are and putting yourself in their position is what will help you, as a leader, to build those personal connections.

CHAPTER 9:
LEVERAGING TEAMS

"When you empower your people, you will have even greater success; and get even more satisfaction from your employees, while at the same time taking yourself to a different level."

As you move into managing and leading at an organizational level, you're not just leading one team any more, you're leading several teams and trying to keep everyone moving in the same direction to accomplish the goals within your organization.

One of the most important talents for leaders to have at this level is the ability to step back, watch those different teams and see how they work. In terms of leveraging your teams to accomplish those goals, I've found cross-functional teams are particularly important.

In any organization, nothing gets done in a vacuum. There are lots of opportunities, if you want to take them, to increase collaboration by creating cross-functional teams that can bring people from across your company together to get things done. However, accomplishing goals and completing tasks is far from the only benefit to establishing cross-functional teams.

Using cross-functional teams to develop people

A bigger reason why we create cross-functional teams at PRECorp is to develop people, give them different experiences and expose them to different people in the organization, which then builds teamwork.

This involves looking beyond the input and output of a particular team. As a leader, you're examining the process of how you put teams together, who you put on those teams and what breadth of cross-functional experience you need. In considering these elements, you will create opportunities for people to develop within those teams.

When you're creating these teams you'll notice that some will really click and do well, while others might struggle. Part of your job, when it comes to leveraging teams, is to be able to look at those who are struggling and diagnose where the issues might be. It's not your job to jump in and fix things, though. Once you're at this level of leadership you will be supporting the leaders of those teams, and the teams themselves, to work through any issues or challenges they encounter.

Mike's leadership lesson: Jenny

Jenny is someone at PRECorp who caught my attention. I noticed that she has a can-do attitude, she wants to get the job done, she takes pride in her work and she wants to make a difference. If she tells you that she's going to do something and makes a commitment, she does not let you down.

Jenny is the type of person who's not afraid to try something new, she's not afraid of change and she's always willing to go the extra mile. She has an incredible ability to internalize a commitment to every member of the team for the duration of a project. If you wanted a team to work well, she is someone you would put on that team, but what was more important was that other people were excited to work with her.

When other people heard that Jenny was on a team, they became excited about the possibility of being on that team too. They wanted to be part of it, feel her energy and clearly they know she's a good team member and enjoy working with her.

My thought was that the more we can expose people to her, the better they're going to get, but also the better she's going to get.

Leadership lessons...

Diagnosing teams isn't only about getting them to accomplish certain tasks, it's about really paying attention to the people who are on each team and how they work together.

When you're in this organizational leadership role, you have to make sure you pay close enough attention to what's going on in your various teams so that you understand how people work together, and can identify who might be natural leaders, whether they're in positions of leadership at this point in their career or not.

When you have that insight, you can leverage teams to not only get the desired output, but to also develop your people and make sure that they're growing, because of the experience they get on that specific team.

Empathy: At this level of leadership, you need to understand both your people and your teams deeply to help them thrive.

Learning by doing

Adults learn best by doing. In the workplace, if you can give someone a project that is not only beneficial to the organization, but that also helps them to grow in some capacity, then that's a huge win for everyone.

"Situational leadership is a model and a construct where we as leaders let go of control. We learn how and when to let go. We shift our thinking and our approach to draw others into leading themselves."

One thing that's very important for leadership development is having a formal and recognized way of developing leaders within your company. First of all, your teams need to know that they're part of something bigger, but you also have to show them that there's a pathway to both leadership and growth within your organization.

At PRECorp, we call this our Action-Based Learning (ABL) group. This is our leadership development program and it's where we take people who have been successful at leading teams in specific areas, to grow their perspective of the company. We want them to see the bigger picture and this is where we take the concept of cross-functional collaboration to the next level and help people grow along the way.

Anyone on our executive team can recommend people to be part of our ABL group and people can also apply directly to join the ABL group themselves. We try to get a team of six to eight together each time the program starts, because we've found this is the sweet spot for this kind of team. These people come from across the organization; we have engineers, people from administration, finance and IT, as well as people who work in the field directly with the infrastructure.

We carry out leadership assessments to decide who to put on the team. These assessments cover intelligence; how they handle conflict; how they think; and, one of the most important factors, their ability to deal with complexity and how far they can envision into the future.

We bring this team together and we ask them to work on one of the big challenges that the company is facing. The problems we give them to solve are the kinds of problems that are the most challenging for any company, because they don't have a right or wrong answer. We give this team one year to work on that specific challenge and we turn them loose on it.

At the end of the year, we have a formal recognition of the end of the program and recognize what they've achieved. At PRECorp, we've found that this process has not only been incredibly successful at developing our people, but also at getting them ready to lead multiple teams.

Delegating

At an organizational level, delegating refers to what I've just been talking about; namely, how to manage all the teams within your organization and get the best from them. This process also involves elements of monitoring and coordinating, which I'll discuss in more detail shortly.

One thing that you have to become very comfortable with when you're leading multiple teams is letting go. This doesn't mean that you don't care where things go, or that you disconnect, but that you trust your people to take care of things.

This can be challenging if you've been used to focusing on leading a single team. When you're just leading one team, you're very hands-on, you're involved in problem solving and you're interfacing with people. When you step up to the next level of leadership, the worst thing you can do is dive in and get in the weeds with people, because then you're taking over.

You have to imagine it as though you're in a car with four people, and all of a sudden you open the door, push the person who's behind the wheel out into the street and start driving. If you do that, everyone else in that car is going to start freaking out. It's the same when you're moving from leading one team to leading multiple teams at an organizational level. You have to be comfortable with allowing someone else to be at the wheel or, in this case, turning over control to your teams.

What really helps, when you start this process of delegating, is that you've done the work I've already talked about – in terms of putting together teams that work, and making sure that they have team charters and know their purpose.

When you start leading multiple teams, you cease to be a player and you move onto the sidelines. Your teams might have problems from time to time, but you have to resist the temptation to jump in and tell everyone how to fix them, even though you might know how.

Instead, you have to coach and guide from the sidelines. You have to tell those people how proud you are of them and how excited you are to see them working on the issues that they're facing. Demonstrating confidence in your teams and their abilities is much more powerful than going in and dealing with issues yourself.

As a leader, you have to be there when your teams need support, which means you ask them questions and you help them clarify their thinking. But the key with delegating at this level is to keep some distance, so you're not involved in solving the day-to-day problems. This leads into another element that's important in terms of leveraging teams, which is monitoring.

Monitoring

There are several ways you can monitor your teams. The most obvious is looking at a team's output and the results they produce. While that's important, monitoring in the context that I'm talking about is more about paying attention to the people on your teams. It's asking them how they are getting on and having frequent conversations with people.

Think back to the driving analogy earlier in the chapter. You're not wresting the steering wheel from someone else's hands, but you're making sure they know that you're there to support them if they need it. You're also avoiding the No-Os of ego, libido and dinero; and instead, focusing on leading with self-awareness and empathy to get the best out of your people.

Putting your energy into the people side of your teams is essential if you want to form high-performing teams within your organization. Your focus needs to be on growing people and leveraging their strengths, rather than on the figures or targets. Everybody knows what those are, but what you often can't see so easily is what's happening behind the scenes, what challenges people are facing and how they work together as a team. This is why monitoring those elements of your teams is so important.

From my perspective, at this level, a leader's job is to serve their team and serve their people. You're there to support their efforts, you're not at the center of the effort. When you think about it in this way, it's clear that monitoring isn't about checking up on your teams. The idea is to use the lightest touch possible to get the most amount of insight into how each team is working. The lighter the touch in this area the better, because the heavier your touch, the more you begin to look like you're the one driving the car.

Mike's leadership lesson: Stepping off the mountain

Strategy has always been something that's been very important to me and, over the years, strategy and vision are areas in which I've become very good. The problem is, when you're good at something, this is often what you love to do; but if you do all of that yourself, you may be neglecting and underutilizing the rest of the team.

When I first started as a CEO, I was not involving the entire team in developing a strategy, instead I would spend time in my office with maybe one or two other people working on a strategy. We'd come up with a great strategy, but then we had to come out of the office, step off our mountain so to speak, and share that strategy with everyone else. People were supportive and gracious, but they could not own it, because it was not theirs. When you work like this, you may, like me, wonder why your teams don't follow through with the strategy or why people struggle with its ownership.

So, we decided to break this model. To do that, we turned the development of a strategy over completely to a series of cross-functional teams within the organization. This meant we essentially involved half the company in developing the strategy. We used the model of scenario planning in this exercise, which means that we set out a potential future and three or four future scenarios. Each of the teams took a scenario to work on.

These scenarios were narrative stories about a possible future for the company. Each team was given complete freedom to develop what their scenario looked like. As CEO, I even delegated the development of the scenarios to my executive staff. Of course, I was coaching them along the way and trying to guide them, but I wasn't in control of the scenarios they developed. That was pretty scary because I had no idea where it was going.

Each member of my executive team then took a particular scenario, formed a cross-functional team and led the team as they worked on that scenario. All of this took the best part of a year. At the end of that period, their job was to paint a picture around the framework of the scenario they had been given to work with.

I didn't know how they would do that or what they would come back with. Each team produced a video that was about 45 minutes long. These videos included scenes that they'd acted out, mock interviews, clips and news that were compelling in their scenario.

We watched these videos together once they were all completed and we were able to see the future of our company in the various scenarios. After seeing those videos, we collectively decided which future we wanted to live as a company. It was pretty obvious which one we all wanted and we decided that this would be the basis of our strategy moving forward.

Leadership lessons...

The first step in this process involved me handing over the reins to my executive team, which really empowered them. This empowerment filtered down through the entire organization.

When you do this, you have to put up with being in a very uncomfortable situation for a while. You might feel frightened that you're not in control, but when you have the courage to turn your teams loose to do the work, you will get incredible passion and buy-in from them.

The output we ended up with from the exercise I described above was amazing. When we decided to translate one of those scenarios into our strategy, everyone at the company bought in 100 percent, because not only did we have half the people within the organization directly working on the scenarios, they also spent a lot of time telling their coworkers what they were doing and how cool it was. That meant everybody saw what was going on and, by the time we got to the point of using those scenarios to crystalize the company's vision and how we would go about executing that strategy, everyone was already on board.

The interesting thing about this example is that the purpose of what we did wasn't actually as much about strategy as it was about developing people. My aim was to find a way to develop my people and to develop leaders. The project I picked to do that through was the strategy.

When you empower your people, you will have even greater success and get even more satisfaction from your employees, while at the same time taking yourself to a different level. Releasing that control can be scary as hell, but it also leads to incredible results for everyone.

Ego and self-awareness: As a leader, you have to be aware of your ego and how it might be making you hold onto control; and you need to have the confidence in your teams to set your ego to one side and allow them to take the reins.

Become the conductor rather than playing in the orchestra

Think of an orchestra. Everybody in the orchestra has their instrument and you have groups of instruments within the orchestra. The conductor stands at the front, where they're conducting the music, maybe pulling more from the strings or more from the brass. They are controlling the tempo and adjusting the musicians to get what they want out of the performance.

The conductor does not go into the orchestra, grab an instrument from somebody and show them how to play it. When you're leveling up, from a leadership perspective, you have to see yourself as the conductor. Obviously, everybody has to be playing off the same sheet of music, and it's your job as the conductor to make sure the musicians have the right music. But you're not using an instrument to create the sound. Instead, it's your job to pull all of those different pieces together to create the sound that you want for a particular performance. You're coordinating all the individuals and teams across your organization to arrive at an end result you all envision. This is a perfect analogy for leveraging teams.

Thinking beyond yourself

The concepts I've talked about in this chapter are about your vision as a leader and how you see your place in the world. This is about thinking beyond yourself and seeing the awesomeness in, and potential for other people.

"If we are going to reach our potential as leaders, we really need to find the courage to change."

In the early days of my time as CEO, I certainly had the tendency to try and grab the wheel from my staff, but they called me out on it. You can see the payoff from me truly relinquishing control to them in the story I shared earlier in this chapter.

In addition to the amazing product that we got out of leveraging teams to think organizationally, how I saw my worth as a leader also changed. Before this exercise, I saw my worth as a leader as being the smartest person in a room filled with the smartest people. I determined my worth as a leader based on knowing all the answers and being able to make all the decisions.

When I let go of that control, I had to find my worth as a leader in a completely different way. Now, I find developing people and helping them to grow and become the best versions of themselves, both at work and in their personal lives, to be much more satisfying than being the smartest guy in the room (or thinking that I'm the smartest guy in the room).

CHAPTER 10: ORGANIZATIONAL THINKING

"To be a really effective leader you have to be able to project your vision out multiple years, especially these days where the world is changing quickly."

As we've progressed through the book, we started by exploring the concept of leading yourself before moving onto leading others in the form of teams. As we get to these higher levels of leadership, it's time to frame your thoughts for thinking organizationally.

When you are thinking organizationally, it's important to recognize that an organization is much greater than the sum of its parts. The process of organizational thinking encompasses several elements. On one level, it's about being able to watch what's happening within your organization and within your teams. On another level, it's the concept of being able to imagine the various futures for your organization to help you understand what you'll have to deal with.

This is much more than simply looking back at the last year of activity within your organization and trying to extrapolate that to predict what the next year will look like. What I'm talking about is being able to understand how your organization fits into the overall landscape of everything that's around you. This goes beyond a business and product sense. It's about looking at what's happening in the world around your organization and examining how those things are having an impact.

You might think of this as seeing the big picture, which is part of it, but it's also about being able to visualize what happens to your organization under future scenarios. These scenarios aren't predicted through your previous performance, they are caused by things happening outside your organization.

To me, that's the key to organizational thinking; being able to see how the environment might be putting pressure on your organization, not just this week and not just next week but, in some cases, years into the future.

To be a really effective leader you have to be able to project your vision out multiple years, especially these days where the world is changing quickly.

Taking organizational thinking beyond you

Being able to take that visioning and strategic thinking beyond the CEO's office is particularly important in this context. If all the visioning and strategic thinking at an organization only happens in the CEO's office then it will only be as good as the CEO.

Sometimes that will be adequate, it might even result in a good plan. The challenge comes when you try to move your organization in that direction. If the visioning and strategic thinking at your organization comes only from you and nobody else, then you have to translate that to the rest of your organization. That will take a lot of time and energy.

What you are aiming for, with your visioning and strategic thinking, is creating strategic alignment within your organization. That means everything and everyone in your organization aligns and focuses on the vision of where the organization needs to go and how it needs to get there. In an ideal world, the people on the front line of your organization will have line of sight clarity for what they're doing and how that impacts the vision of the company.

If you can create that line of sight, so that every person in your organization knows how they contribute to the overall vision and strategy of the organization, then they become empowered to achieve it and they will help you move that strategy forward. The issue is that, when you create that strategy alone and then try to deliver it to the masses from on high, you give yourself a ton of work to do.

What really helps with visioning is to think about your organization in terms of the relationships and people who all do different things within it. As a leader, you want to think about how you can align all those conversations and actions; and getting everyone involved from the ground level up really helps, as demonstrated in the story I shared in the last chapter.

Mike's leadership lesson: Strategic alignment

When I was completing my MBA, one of the projects we covered was the process of creating strategic alignment in the organization. For this project, I created a strategic alignment model of the organization. I easily spent 100 hours putting together this really great mind map that showed all the links between the departments and the people, and how you could align them along performance, communication and even messaging to our members. I was so proud of myself.

I brought this model of how to create strategic alignment within the organization back to my staff and sat down with them to explain the model. Everybody was very polite, as they typically are when a CEO comes down from on high and pontificates, and they tried to embrace it and make it work. We had varying levels of success, depending on people's ability to understand the complexity of where things were going and how they were related.

We spent two years trying to align the company to this strategy, but we could never quite get it to work in the way I wanted it to. At the time, I was pretty frustrated and I stepped back from that approach to find a new way forward. I told you about this project in Chapter 9, where I handed over the scenario planning to my teams.

As you saw in the last chapter, that approach was incredibly successful and resulted in tremendous buy-in across the organization.

Leadership lessons...

Strategy consultants will tell you that strategy is everyone's business. What they won't tell you, however, is that if you want it to be everyone's business, it has to be their business from day one.

This was what we achieved by using cross-functional teams to carry out the scenario planning and to use this to inform our strategy for the future. We also found a way that everyone in the organization could be involved in creating that future vision for our company. We did that by setting up a virtual data center and encouraging everyone to contribute to it.

Self-awareness: As a leader, you need to be able to see when your approach is not working as well as it could, and have the humility to admit this and find another, better way forward. It is important that you are able to let go of ideas that are not working for the team, even ones that you are in love with.

Involving everyone in landscape analysis

As I mentioned, we set up a data center and the idea was that anyone in the company could add articles or information to it that was relevant to the organization. In our case, that meant anything to do with energy, Wyoming, and regulations that could impact the business, among others.

As well as pushing this out to our entire team, we also invited people outside the organization to help us create this huge data center. While we were collecting this data, we had a team of people who were labeling articles and adding metadata to enable us to sort all this information that we were collecting.

After a few weeks of collecting data, we parsed it down into themes. Once we had those, we asked people to take a deep dive into these articles and create summaries and takeaways. This is what we call landscape analysis.

The result was that, among about 50 people within the organization, we had a pretty clear idea of what the landscape was and where things were heading. Using all the threads of information that we'd pulled together in our data center, we created a tapestry of what our future environment was likely to look like.

At this point, we brought everybody together and started exploring various "What if?" scenarios. This was an exercise we carried out seven or eight years ago, and one of the major questions we asked ourselves then was, "What if the energy pivots away from hydrocarbon energy? How does that impact us?"

In our position, that was a pretty scary scenario because our company is a co-op. Co-ops nationally are very heavily invested in the use of coal because, around 50 years ago, whenever co-ops were starting to build power supply, it was illegal in the US to use natural gas to generate electricity. The reason being that there were concerns we'd run out of natural gas, and that was needed to heat homes.

As a result, co-ops across the U.S. invested heavily in coal. A lot of that infrastructure is in the co-op's portfolio, so imagining what happens when that goes away is scary. We forced ourselves to consider that through our scenarios and, if you fast forward to today, you can see that coal use is dropping off extremely fast. There are even discussions globally about peak oil demand having been reached, and we really saw that in 2020, with people moving away from driving and traveling, in general.

We started imagining this future way back in 2012-13, and we were asking ourselves, "If that future is going to come, what are some of the things we need to do to be ready for it?"

Another scenario we looked at was a very high penetration of electric cars and what we would need to do to meet that scenario. We also considered fires and how we would deal with a big fire running through our system, as well as what we would have to do to be ready for that possibility.

Pulling out the common threads

Those are just a few examples of the scenarios that we used in our vision. From this exercise, we were left with a list of all the things we could do. At this point, we stepped back and asked, "What are the common steps we, as a company, need to be taking, no matter what happens to us under these scenarios?"

Those common threads then highlighted the competencies we needed, the actions we needed to take and the procedures and processes we needed to be working on to ensure we were resilient, and able to deal with any one of those numerous scenarios that could come down the pipe.

These common elements became our strategy for how to have a good company going forward. They informed our vision and helped us to adjust our purpose to enable us to be successful moving onwards.

The ideas of developing and growing our leadership, as well as focusing on our culture, were the common elements we saw as being essential to the future of the company. One of the most important was having good leadership in the company.

We want to have leaders who are comfortable in uncertainty, as well as leaders who are very self-aware, not only in terms of understanding their own performance, but also how they impact the people around them. These are essentially the cornerstones of our visioning and strategic-thinking activity.

Because we had involved so many people from across the company from the beginning, when we began the process of rolling out and formally developing our strategy and its supporting mechanisms, everybody already knew about it. We didn't have to spend time and energy bringing them to where we were, or asking them to trust us. Instead, they were already there and actually anxiously awaiting the outcomes of our strategic planning and thinking process to enable them to start working on our various initiatives.

Through this process, not only did our leaders understand that the organization is bigger than the sum of its parts and the importance of preparing it to respond to an uncertain future, but a large number of our employees also had this understanding. That meant we were able to create buy-in and move things forward pretty quickly. The outcome here, compared to when I came back to the organization with my awesome mind map, was completely different.

How to involve people in visioning and strategic thinking

When you start discussing how you can involve as many people as possible in your organization's strategic thinking and visioning process, your biggest limitation in terms of resources is likely to be time. Ideally, you want to involve as many people as your organization can afford to involve.

You can certainly do that strategically, starting by looking at your high potentials on the frontline, all the way up to the C-suite managers. When you bring these people together and get them to contribute to your strategy process in the way I outlined above, several things happen.

First, you're getting an output in terms of a strategy or a strategy process that you're ready to launch to the wider organization. Secondly, you're launching this strategy with a bunch of supporters because they have been part of the process. Finally, you're developing your people. This is a really important by-product of this approach.

Just by virtue of people being part of this process, working together in cross-functional teams and looking at some of the challenges facing your organization, they are developing their own abilities to think strategically and on this organizational level. You are giving them the gift of a huge amount of professional training that will keep giving back to you, because now you have this group of people who understand the bigger picture and as a result, you'll see better leaders coming through your organization in the long run.

Developing your own strategic thinking

To start developing your own strategic thinking, it's important to understand what this is, and what it is not. For me, it comes down to understanding the difference between strategic thinking and operational thinking.

Strategic thinking is thinking about things that add new value to the organization or process, whereas operational thinking is preserving the status quo or preserving value. Operational thinking is, of course, important for leaders, but strategic thinking is really what you need to move your organization to the next level.

What you'll find the higher you go in an organization's leadership, and the more responsibility you have, is that you'll spend more and more time in this strategic frame of mind; where you're searching for ideas that can create new value for your organization. To do this you have to be able to step outside yourself and step outside your organization.

This is an ongoing process, rather than a one-time event, and understanding that aspect of strategic thinking is hugely important. Ultimately, strategic thinking leads you to strategy and from there you have to execute that strategy, which in itself becomes a process and discipline.

Be future focused

One of the most important aspects of strategic thinking is that you're looking to the future. Earlier in the book, I used the analogy of a car and its headlights. When you're a leader at this level of an organization, you need your headlights to be on bright, like when you're driving at night. You're seeing a little bit around the bend and trying to anticipate the potential issues just over the horizon to make sure your organization is ready for them.

The vision you have for the organization is central to this. It's the reason for your company's existence and it should, therefore, be a focal point that you can use to inspire your company and move your people to understand how their job is contributing to that greater purpose, and how they personally are adding value.

Once your people start to see how their daily work contributes to something bigger than themselves, you have the ability to involve more than just their day-to-day activities. You start to involve their cognitive resources and their passions. At this point, you start to tap into some of their discretionary time, thoughts and energy, which truly is of great value to the company.

The way that strategic thinking ties into this vision from your perspective is that, while you're giving people this compelling vision that they can identify with and work towards, you also need to break that vision down into what you're going to do to achieve it.

This is your strategy; it's how you're going to get there. Within that strategy, there will be various initiatives that the company is going to take on to deliver on that vision and, ultimately, achieve it.

The idea of strategy needs to be developed and run just like it's project management. You have your vision, you turn that into an executable strategy and then you execute the strategy. You measure the results and make adjustments where you need to. This is a continuous process.

Where many companies fall down is that they produce a strategic plan in a big thick binder that then gets put on a shelf somewhere and forgotten. You don't need the thick ring binder for your strategy. It's far more important that you are able to communicate it to people, both those within your organization and your vendors and stakeholders. I would advise you to think of your strategy in the terms of a one-page elevator pitch; because in condensing it you can communicate it, engage people with it and start working on it.

Applied organizational thinking

The background

The Powder River Energy Corporation (PRECorp) is a member-owned electrical cooperative providing service to over 12,000 members in Northeast Wyoming. In 2007, there was a tremendous boom in energy development in the region, which led to the largest increase in demand that PRECorp had ever faced. The challenge was to scale fast enough to meet this demand.

Pain points

PRECorp struggled to meet this rapid increase in demand. Connections to the grid lagged behind schedule. The company's internal processes were insufficient to meet the high-volume demands and were inconsistent across its three office locations. Employees lacked adequate training and smooth direction from managers. It quickly became apparent that the business needed to adapt its operations to keep up with the changing market.

Solutions

At PRECorp, we chose to use the Palladium Execution Premium Process™ to drive alignment, not only across the organizational business units and offices, but also within our internal teams and external members. The way we approached each of these challenges varied depending on the group we wanted to reach.

Members: We focused heavily on communication. This involved producing a monthly newsletter and inviting our members to share their concerns and ask questions about our strategy. These "pain points" were translated into performance measures that we could actively track and improve at PRECorp.

Offices and business units: We defined clear, cooperative-wide measures and processes by bringing different departments together to review and discuss the best ways to conduct and measure our various processes. We also identified the strategic measures that are used as part of our Balanced Scorecards (BSC).

People: We used the BSC and tied individual employee goals and personal development plans to PRECorp objectives. We made it as simple as possible for people to track and review their progress using personal scorecards. We engaged our employees in scenario-planning exercises, and asked them to examine PRECorp's core values from internal, member and community perspectives.

The outcomes

· PRECorp's customer satisfaction score was 3.6 percent higher than its cooperative peers and 11 percent higher than investor-owned utilities.

· There was greater clarity around PRECorp's performance expectations.

· In 2013, an average of five personal goals were set per employee.

· Performance incentives were linked to both cooperative performance and scores on individual performance reviews.

· Employee motivation and strategic understanding was improved.

· There were a number of material improvements between 2008 and 2013 as a direct result of this work.

· The work order closeout process time decreased 93 percent, from three years to 70 days.

· Outage duration (SAIDI) decreased 57 percent, from 200 minutes to 86 minutes.

- Construction time frames decreased 69 percent for residential members, and 64 percent for commercial members.

- Employee personal scorecard participation and completion increased from 77 percent to 90 percent.

You can read the PRECorp case study at: noosofleadership.com/precorpcasestudy

Building on success

This case study illustrates what was happening at PRECorp in 2008–2013, but fast forward several years and what we learned about strategy and involving your team was very compelling. Our most recent strategic update at PRECorp included nearly half of our team in developing our strategy.

As we have executed that strategy and continue to do so, one of the things we have learned is everybody in the company has big ownership of the strategy, and we have stayed incredibly focused on the strategy throughout the Covid-19 pandemic. At the time of writing this, we had recently completed an employee opinion survey, which found 99 percent of our employees agreed or strongly agreed, they were very clear about their goals and the organizational strategy. This survey also returned a similar overall employee satisfaction score.

What this demonstrates is that there is a great opportunity to align strategy and capture the hearts and minds of your employees by involving them in the early stages of developing your organizational strategy, and as deeply as your organization can afford to.

CHAPTER 11: THE NO-OS OF LEADERSHIP

"Being cognizant of the No-Os of leadership and checking your behavior, decision making and thinking against them will make you a better leader; one who is easier to follow."

Over the course of my professional career, I've had the opportunity to work under many different leaders. At the same time, I've always been a student of leadership and am always working to become a better leader. I've sought to understand what makes good leaders and what makes bad leaders.

I would see leaders who I knew experiencing leadership failures and I would also see leaders who are in the public eye, such as presidents, politicians and other high-profile figureheads, experiencing leadership failures. One day they would be on top of the world, the next they would be gone. I started observing these leadership failures, being astute and always seeking to understand what had happened, because I wanted to be a good leader and avoid those kinds of failures.

What came out of this observation isn't a scientific study, but it led me to the No-Os of Leadership. As I said in the introduction to Part 3, these No-Os are ego, libido, dinero.

I've talked about how important it is for leaders to be self-aware, and whenever I'm coaching leaders and discussing problems and challenges, one of the areas I talk about with them is epic leadership failures. What I've noticed is that, if you're in a situation where one of those No-Os is activated, you're on dangerous ground. These are big red flags that you, as a leader, need to be thinking about and aware of.

Ego failures in leadership

An ego failure in leadership is when a leader is blind to themselves. They make decisions that are all about themselves, not about their people. I'm not saying that good leaders should have no ego, but we have to have humility and be humble. If you make a mistake, you have to take responsibility and not blame it on other people. Making a mistake and blaming it on everyone else is a clear sign of an ego issue. As Ken Blanchard says, "Great leaders don't think less of themselves, they just think about themselves less."

It boils down to the signals we send to our people. For example, as the leader, do you have the best parking space right by the front door to the building? You might have it for a reason, because you're always coming to work late or you're in and out all the time, but do you always have to park there? And if someone else parks in that space by the front door, do you get mad about it? Do you feel angry or stressed if that happens? Could you instead think, "I'm sure they were in a hurry" or "I need a walk today"? That's just a very small example of how, as a leader, you can not lead with your ego.

Ego also means being blind to your weaknesses and the overextension of power as a leader. Ego tends to feed and create even more challenges for the No-O of libido, which we'll talk about later. Ego manifests in a lot of ways in leadership; it's an assumption that no matter what you do or think, you're right and that the wake you create through your actions is of no consequence.

There are lots of examples of ego failures in politics. In fact, I don't think a person can be a successful politician without having a very strong sense of self and a very strong ego. However, where I think it can go awry is when politicians and leaders don't pay attention to their wake and the impact of their ego on others.

 # Mike's leadership lesson: Electing the 46th president of the U.S.

On November 3, 2020 the U.S. public went to the polls in what was one of the most anticipated and talked about presidential elections in recent history. Donald Trump was campaigning for a second term. Joe Biden had the Democratic ticket. In the lead up to the election, the polls were inconclusive. In the days after the polls closed, there was little else on the news other than which of the candidates had won which states and the associated electoral college votes.

Eventually, Joe Biden was declared the winner and named as the 46th president of America. But, something remarkable happened in those days following the election. Incumbent Donald Trump refused to concede the election. He peddled stories about voter fraud, despite credible evidence to the contrary.

His insistent narrative that the election had been "stolen" from him led to a huge demonstration and the country's Capitol being overrun as a joint session of Congress met to formalize Joe Biden's victory and election as the U.S. president.

Leadership lessons...

The group of Trump supporters who gathered at the Capitol that day, intent on disrupting the count of electoral college votes, were there as a result of Donald Trump's failure to concede the election and his inability to see what the wake of that decision might be. The flip side, of course, is that he was fully aware of his wake and that this was the outcome he intended, which is even worse.

Donald Trump's ego prevented him from accepting that he could be wrong. The resulting wake from his decision can be seen clearly in the images and news reports of what happened on January 6, 2021.

Of course, we'll never know for sure whether Trump conceding the election would have prevented this demonstration and subsequent riot from taking place. However, I think many would argue it would certainly have been a smaller, less-impactful demonstration, at the very least, had Trump walked away from the White House gracefully, rather than allowing his ego to blind him to the truth of what was happening.

Ego: As a leader you have to accept that you can be wrong and, when you are, to be humble enough to take responsibility for that, as well as any outcomes that your wrong decision may have caused.

Dinero failures in leadership

It seems in today's world that money is a huge motivator. One of the things I learned from Ken Blanchard is the concept of the triple bottom line. This refers to happy employees, happy customers, and the revenue that comes in being the applause of both of those things, without being the primary driver. Dinero can show up in how we run and focus our businesses.

We know businesses need to make money to be successful. Dinero isn't about making money in that sense. What I'm talking about is making decisions that are solely intended to benefit you (or the business) from a financial perspective, without consideration of your employees or customers. When that happens, it's a problem.

Dinero failures can also show up in leaders who make decisions to enrich themselves at the expense of their employees and their members or customers. For example, I haven't seen a corporate bankruptcy filing that doesn't give the executive team huge bonuses and a huge payout early on. That's usually explained away by saying that these are key people who are needed to run the organization while it's restructured. However, I tend to think that if leaders have their dinero in check, they would have a sense of responsibility to their employees and their customers; and would, therefore, feel less entitled to large bonuses when things are going badly, and be more motivated to do the right thing and take care of their employees and customers.

Mike's leadership lesson:
Money tricks

Joe was 17 and looking for a job. He found one with Steve, who ran the local auto shop. Although Joe didn't fully understand all the ins and outs of business, one thing he did register about Steve was that he seemed to be more concerned about money than he was about taking care of people and doing the right thing.

Joe quickly learned that if Steve was able to take a used part, and make it as good as new, he would charge customers for a new part. The other mechanics used to quietly shake their heads at this practice, but they all needed their jobs so none of them spoke up.

One of the older mechanics even told Joe that Steve didn't use to play these tricks, but that once he had accidentally charged a customer for a new part, rather than a used one that had been repaired, and the customer hadn't noticed it. Steve had realized he could make a bit of extra money here and there with this, so instead of seeing it as a one-off occurrence it became a part of his operations.

One day, Steve took Joe to the side and asked him to help catch an error at the bank. He wrote Joe a check for $250 and told him that if he went to the bank and cashed it, he could keep $50 and just give $200 back. This happened reasonably frequently, and it took Joe years before he understood that Steve was actually using him to get money from his operating loans.

The problem was, the more Steve behaved in a shady manner, the more his business struggled and the more he turned to underhanded practices to make up the difference. Like many of the mechanics who worked there, Joe felt uneasy and after a couple of years left for another job. None of them felt as though they could say anything to Steve or stand up to him. Eventually, Steve's auto shop went out of business, despite the fact that he always had good mechanics working for him.

Leadership lessons...

Steve wasn't a bad person, but he didn't always do the right thing and was often motivated to make decisions based on his financial gain, going against the dinero No-O of leadership. However, his leadership failures started off as small things. In fact, the first time he sold a used part as a new part, it was a mistake.

But Steve never challenged his leadership against the No-Os. He didn't stop to ask whether his decisions were being driven by his own financial gain, rather than what was best for his customers. He wasn't transparent about his operations and, ultimately, that resulted in him losing business.

Steve also failed in his leadership in that he put his team in a difficult position where they were unable to stand up to the practices they disagreed with. Throughout my career I have certainly seen people do shady things and it can be easy to wonder why no one speaks up when you're on the outside looking in. However, it is very difficult to stand up and say something when you are not in a position of power within an organization.

There are also leadership lessons from a self-leadership perspective in Joe and Steve's story. Wherever you are on your leadership journey, it's important to test your decisions against those No-Os of leadership. Ask yourself questions like: Are you getting a personal reward from a situation? Does a situation unfairly advantage you from a monetary perspective? You might not feel as though you have the power to stand up to poor leadership where you are now, but you can always lead yourself according to those standards. Joe did, which is why he left to find another job.

Dinero: As leaders, we know that being financially strong is important for any organization, but it's better to approach decision making from the perspective of serving your members or team than purely from financial motives.

Organizations go through financial stress; at these times they make cuts and they make changes. If you, as the leader of the company, aren't leading by example and taking those cuts yourself, whether that's to your bonus or your compensation, then that will create problems because people will find out.

If you're considering pay cuts in your organization, you'd better cut your wages a year before you cut anybody else's, and don't tell anybody about it. That will mean the year that you implement those pay cuts you can say, "I've already been doing this for a year myself." People will respect that.

Libido failures in leadership

As a leader, it's important to really understand your relationship with leadership and, in this context, there are three components: passion, commitment and intimacy. As a leader, intimacy means knowing yourself and being able to face your weaknesses and identify areas you could improve. This also involves having the willingness and desire to address any faults you do see. Commitment in this context is in terms of your relationship with yourself as a leader. It's about remembering who you are, what's important to you and what values you identified in your leadership point of view. These three elements – passion, commitment and intimacy – need to be a balanced triangle.

Libido can be a leadership challenge when the passion side of your relationship with leadership is out of balance. So, if you focus overly on passion as a leader and don't balance that out with commitment and intimacy, your libido could go unchecked.

If we're honest with ourselves, I think we can agree that we have either experienced or caused other people to experience an unchecked libido in the context of our passion being out of control. Organizationally, I've been in a position where something has really upset me and my passion and emotions are very heightened. I can remember sitting down early in my career when I was in this state, to write the kind of scathing email that puts the other person down and elevates me. Can you identify with this? You hit send, but you don't get to take those emails back. Those emails can be damaging to the individual you send them to, and to your team.

Mostly, when you release that passion into the workplace without carefully considering the message that you're sending, the position that you're taking and how you're using your power as a leader, what you're really doing is setting an example of what happens when you have an unchecked libido, and that has no place in the workplace.

When you look at the leadership failures that we have seen in the world when that passion becomes sexual in nature, those are often what could be described as epic leadership failures. I'm not trying to make a moral statement with the idea of libido, but if you look at the disruption that happens in an organization when a leader has an unchecked libido, it's pretty crazy.

There was a story in the U.S. in 2009 about a state governor who went missing. For six days, his whereabouts were unknown. There was, of course, a great deal of speculation in the press. His spokesperson said that he was "hiking the Appalachian Trail", while questions were raised about who was acting as governor of South Carolina in his absence. When he reappeared, it turned out he had been on vacation in Buenos Aires with a woman who was not his wife. He was, of course, having an affair, which all came to light shortly after he came back from the trip. It also transpired that this was not the first time he had engaged in an extramarital affair. Due to both political and voter pressure, he had to resign.

We also saw this with Bill Clinton and his affair with Monica Lewinsky. In that story there was also ego involved, so two of the No-Os. That didn't completely take him down, but it severely impacted his presidency and the country as a whole.

Most recently, Andrew Cuomo, the Governor of New York resigned amidst numerous sexual harassment allegations. Governor Cuomo and his administration enjoyed numerous political successes during his tenure.

How many times have you seen a story in the news about a leader who has done something like send inappropriate photos to someone from their phone? Every time I see those stories, I see them as leadership failures.

Mike's leadership lesson: Hank and Rick

Hank put his head in his hands as Charlotte turned on her heel and left the office, slamming the door behind her. It didn't take long before Rick popped his head in. "I'm guessing Charlotte's not working her shift tomorrow?" Hank sighed. "No, she quit," he said. Rick shrugged. "Oh well, I think I know someone who might be able to fill in..." With that he left the office, and Hank just thought, *here we go again!*

In the early years of the convenience store boom in the U.S., Hank and Rick saw an opportunity to run a really great business. Both of them were in college studying for their Masters degrees. Hank was studying business and Rick was studying psychology.

From the early days, Hank focused on the business and how it was run behind the scenes. He looked after the money, inventory and all those aspects of the store. Rick, meanwhile, took care of hiring staff and dealing with customers.

However, gradually it became clear that Rick was hiring women that he liked and, over time, would start dating them. This made the dynamic among the staff strange and after a while there was a collective sigh of, "this is the next one". Hank could always tell when things were starting to sour in the relationship, because the woman would be unusually quiet at work, or start phoning in sick for shifts here and there. Then, when the relationship ended, that woman would quit and the cycle would usually start again.

Hank tried to build up the courage to speak to Rick about it, but he always lost his nerve. He was introverted and hated conflict, and that made him reluctant to talk to Rick about his behavior.

He told himself that if he behaved in an exemplary, professional way, that would help. He led by example and tried to make up for the damage Rick caused, but he was never able to balance everything out. Over time, Hank became resentful. He felt as though he put everything into the business, when all Rick did was take from it. Gradually, Hank and Rick's relationship became fractured and eventually their partnership broke down, which also saw the end of what had been a successful business and what would have been an incredible opportunity.

Leadership lessons...

Many of us have worked in businesses with more than one manager, and what I learned very early on in my working life is that good leaders put in more than they take out of a business. On the face of it, Hank and Rick had very complementary skills and knowledge with their respective backgrounds in business and psychology.

However, Rick was using the business to serve himself, whereas Hank focused on the business and always tried to do the right thing. In the end, they were incompatible. Rick's leadership failures related to libido and although he may not have started out with the intention of basing his hiring decisions on whether he was attracted to the women applying, this became a pattern of behavior.

We tend to make mistakes in small steps and we also tend to accept dysfunction a little bit at a time. On a personal level, having awareness of the No-Os and being able to recognize their impact on your own leadership decisions can really help you to stay on the right track and alter your decisions to become a better leader. If you notice any one of the No-Os influencing your leadership decisions, know that it's never too late to change, but also that you have to change.

Although it was Rick's behavior that caused the biggest issues at the convenience store, Hank also didn't help this situation. Like many people, he wanted to avoid conflict and because he was afraid to speak up or hurt Rick's feelings, he didn't communicate his concerns or frustrations with Rick. Hank's leadership failure might also be seen in the light of a No-Os failure, albeit a very subtle one. Hank was very worried about his image of being a nice and personable guy. His failure was one of ego. Not about having an overly large ego, but an ego preoccupied with a seemingly helpful self-image. Hank's ego was overly protecting him from negative feelings associated with thinking that people might not see him as a personable and pleasant leader.

You have to remember that the only thing you can change is yourself. If you're part of a business partnership where you are giving and the other person is taking, you have to start by looking at your approach to communication. Are you having open and honest conversations, or are you being passive-aggressive, dropping hints and becoming increasingly frustrated that nothing is changing?

If it's the latter, you have to think about what you can do differently in terms of how you're communicating, because your hesitation to directly engage is part of the problem.

If you are having those frank conversations, however, and still nothing is changing, then you have to get out of that partnership. You have to accept that you are the only person that you can change in any situation, and sometimes that means walking away.

Libido and ego: You can't allow your passions to rule your decisions and behavior as a leader. Equally, you have to make sure you're not feeding into someone else's leadership failures by failing to take action yourself.

It's important to note that libido isn't restricted to its sexual context. It's also about how we use our power over other people. It can also refer to instances where someone is sucking power away from someone else.

If we look at Donald Trump, and I'm not going to throw stones at him from a political perspective, I think you can see that all three No-Os – ego, libido and dinero – are issues there, and when I look at that through a leadership lens, that's failed leadership.

When the three No-Os are unrestrained in how you lead, I just don't think you can be effective. You might have short-term success, or you might have enough power and gravitas to lead for a time, but you won't find long-term leadership success.

Leaving a legacy

Leadership, for me, is influencing people and ensuring that your time at the helm leaves a team, a department or an organization better than when you found it. Your legacy doesn't have to be anything huge, it simply has to be that you left things better than you found them.

Being cognizant of the No-Os of leadership and checking your behavior, decision making and thinking against them will make you a better leader; one who is easier to follow. Your people will have more loyalty and respect for you and, ultimately, your organization or your team will perform better over time.

The No-Os of leadership aren't about casting judgments. They are there to guide you. When you're making decisions, decide what kind of leader you want to be. Nobody is going to decide they want to be an egotistical leader. Nobody is going to say they want to be a leader so they can take financial advantage of others. Nobody is going to say they want to be a leader who takes advantage of people or who abuses their position of power.

As you go through life and encounter situations, it's important to have awareness of ego, libido and dinero as potential landmines that you, as a leader, can step in. If you have that awareness, you have a much better chance of navigating your leadership journey without setting off those landmines.

This brings us full circle to self-awareness and taking the time to reflect so that you can understand situations and reactions. This gives you the time to self-regulate and side-step the landmines of the No-Os.

These are three areas where I've seen many leaders fail. If you want to lead well over time, you need to have respect for your people; and if you're not checking yourself on the No-Os, you won't have that respect for them and, as a consequence, they won't respect you.

CHAPTER 12: THE MAGIC OF THE BOARDROOM

"When you become CEO, it's important to remember that you are the physical embodiment of the board's decision and with that comes awesome responsibilities and amazing opportunities."

In this final chapter, I'd like to focus specifically on how CEOs of cooperatives can work more effectively with their boards. Having said that, what I share here has applications for anyone working for a board of directors, be it in a non-profit or a private company. I'm going to use the term CEO throughout, although in your organization your title could be manager, general manager or even executive director. Please take CEO as a term that encompasses all of these.

One thing to keep in mind throughout this discussion about working with boards is that one of the most, if not the most, important decisions a board of directors makes is who they hire as CEO. This is because you, as the CEO, are the walking embodiment of the board's decision. As a result, there is a significant amount of responsibility, not only due to your position but also because how you interact with your team and company, your stakeholders and your board is a reflection of the board's decision and their faith and trust in you. As you read this chapter, I would like you to keep this in mind, along with the No-Os of leadership: ego, libido and dinero. The decisions you make as a CEO, as well as the decisions made in the boardroom, would do well to be tested by the No-Os of leadership.

I hope that this chapter will give you some insight into working with boards and that the stories I share are helpful to you on your leadership journey.

The mystique of the boardroom

In a professional context, my first experience of boards was quite early in my career through board meetings at the cooperative I worked for. These board meetings typically happened once a month and on that particular day (and even throughout the week) the whole atmosphere of the organization changed – people dressed up in nicer clothes and appeared to be a little more serious in their day-to-day work. As someone new in that organization, it was very obvious to me that something important was happening, not only in the boardroom on the "upper" floor, but throughout the whole organization. The whole event was shrouded in a sense of mystique.

This experience gave me a very healthy respect for the boardroom and the board members themselves. I can clearly remember the first day I had the opportunity to go to the "upper" floor at the cooperative headquarters because I had a meeting with one of the senior executives. I can still hear the "swish" as the elevator doors opened and remember looking out and noticing that the office was furnished a little differently; there was even a distinctive aroma to this important and impressive space. As I stepped out of the elevator, the carpet felt so thick and deep that I imagined it was swelling up around my ankles. I felt honored (and also a little scared) to be walking the hallways where the board of directors and senior executives worked.

This particular day was a pivotal moment in my career. My meeting with the senior executive was successful and, as a result, I was given more responsibility in the work I was doing, which set me on a different and exciting trajectory within that organization and marked the start of my leadership journey.

The sense of mystique surrounding boards is not an uncommon one and, in fact, I believe it is justified because many important decisions and issues get played out in boardrooms. As leaders, we should never forget that when the board has convened, all the people on that board are acting as a unified voice to direct the affairs of the cooperative and set policy. It is a special time and a special place.

We should all keep this in the back of our minds, no matter how familiar we are with what happens in the boardroom and no matter how long we have been a CEO. It's truly an honor to be in the position to serve a board that, in the case of electric cooperatives, represents the member owners of the organization.

Building relationships with boards

As my career progressed, I had the opportunity to have a presence at board meetings and I watched several CEOs interact with their board members and, of course, watched those board members interact with the CEOs. Through this process, I could see the value in this relationship and worked to understand this relationship between the board and the CEO. I realized that it involves a continual building of trust between both the board and the CEO. When this relationship is built correctly over time, it has a significant overall benefit for the organization and the service it delivers to its members.

However, when this relationship is not built correctly it can lead to growing feelings of mistrust and anxiety. This tone doesn't only extend to the board-CEO relationship; it will find its way throughout the entire organization and impact the way people interact with each other and the leaders within the organization. Therefore, it's critical that the CEO and the board find a way to work together and continually build trust in each other and the organization for the benefit of everyone – employees and the membership.

When you come into work as a CEO at a cooperative, you will be serving your members by faithfully executing your duties as a CEO. One of those duties is to work well with the board and this not only means building a strong relationship with them, but also understanding what they do and their role in your community.

Understanding the role of the board of directors

To build this trust as a CEO, you need to understand the role of the board of directors and have a healthy respect for what they bring to the table. In the world of electric cooperatives, board members will often have strong ties to the community and it is these ties that have established them as community leaders and helped them get elected to a board seat.

However, oftentimes those ties to the community go much deeper than a CEO may realize or understand at first blush. Particularly in small cooperatives and those in rural areas, board members may have been serving for decades. They may have been elected to the board at a very young age and, in some cases, could perhaps have been on the board as long as the CEO themselves has been in the cooperative business.

Many board members will therefore have very strong and intimate ties to the community and the cooperative's membership. There are usually fairly strong relationships between board members and employees as well, because many of the employees at cooperatives have been there for many years. Some of the board members and employees may even have grown up together in the town or service territory for the cooperative, which means it has been part of both their and their families' lives. Many of these families have been part of the cooperative for generations.

As a CEO, it is important to be very considerate of those relationships because of the potential closeness between the board and the members, as well as between the board and the employees. When a CEO fails to understand and consider these strong, close relationships, opportunities for conflict arise.

The board makes the decision about who to hire as the CEO. Once they have made that decision, they are looking for feedback to validate that decision and to understand whether this was the best decision for the cooperative. When they are looking for this validation, there will more than likely be conversations between the board members and members of the cooperative, as well as between board members and some of the employees.

While this is an opportunity for the board and the CEO to build trust, it is also an opportunity for conflict to arise if the CEO perceives the conversations between employees and board members to violate the chain of command in the organization. If the CEO sees these conversations as a threat, their ego may kick in and the CEO may become defensive. When that happens, the result is typically not a positive trust-building experience.

Mike's leadership lesson: New kid on the block

When I arrived at PRECorp as their new CEO over 21 years ago, I was figuratively and literally "the new kid on the block". The cooperative was going through a very challenging time and the board hired me because of my fresh perspective of the issues and my ability to articulate a compelling vision. I also knew some things had to change.

These changes were very scary for many people on the PRECorp team at that time. I commissioned an employee survey and I will never forget the painful comments from some of the employees, and in particular the one about the company needing a real CEO, not an apprentice CEO, cut pretty deep. I shared all these comments with the board and they supported me, as well as challenged me, to build the relationships and the trust I needed to be successful.

It also became apparent that employees were expressing concerns to the board and this was creating some difficulties for everyone. We decided to set some boundaries in how we dealt with this type of dialogue. We wanted the balance between having one's finger on the pulse of the organization and ensuring that dialogue was productive and transparent.

Leadership lessons...

Both myself and the board recognized the value of this dialogue between the board and the employees at the cooperative, so we didn't try to squash it. Instead, we agreed how best to gather that feedback and how it would be shared with me.

If an employee came to the board with some feedback, they would listen carefully to what they had to say and then ask, "Have you talked to Mike about that?" Usually the employee would say, "No" and they would be redirected to me. Often that would be done gently with a suggestion like, "The operational stuff is Mike's responsibility, so you need to talk to him about it." They also reassured the employee that this issue was on their radar. One of the board members would then call me to give me a heads-up about the issue I needed to have awareness of and to give me time to think about how best to deal with it.

Ego and self-awareness: You have to put down your ego in this situation, be vulnerable and accept feedback, wherever it comes from. You also have to be grateful for that feedback and self-aware enough to see how it can help you develop on your leadership journey.

As you can see from my story, to prevent this scenario from occurring, it's important that both the board and the CEO understand their areas of responsibility and the chain of command. As the CEO, you have to look at conversations between employees and board members, not as a threat to you or the chain of command, but as opportunities to gather data and information about the team and then consider how you can use the information to better serve the team, the membership and the board.

The CEO and board members may need to have some very important conversations to reach this level of understanding. Regardless of an individual board member's relationship with an employee or group of employees, when the board is operating as a whole alongside the manager, the outcome will be that these conversations are seen as a unique way to gather input to help make things better, while keeping the chain of command in mind. What you want to avoid are these conversations between board members and employees resulting in the board directing or demanding action from the CEO.

The best method I have seen to ensure these conversations are used constructively is for these interactions to be presented to the board and the CEO as information. Based upon that information, the CEO can take action to address potential issues or to gain greater insight into what might be happening in the organization.

When used in this way, the outcome of having this information is to make the cooperative stronger and better. It also builds trust with the board, because approaching the information in this way demonstrates that the manager is confident enough in what they do that they don't see this dialogue as a threat. It also enables healthy and robust conversations between the manager and the board to happen to ensure that everybody knows the areas of their responsibility.

Typically that will mean the board of directors is setting policy, helping to make important strategic decisions, setting guidelines and boundaries; and then facilitating and supporting the CEO and management team as they execute that strategy within the boundaries of the policies that have been set.

Mike's leadership lesson: Creating a positive culture of communication

As I mentioned in the previous story, when I came to PRECorp as CEO, the cooperative was going through some very significant growing pains and transition because of things that had happened prior to my arrival. There had been a merger which, while completed from the perspective of the organizational name, balance sheet and broader entity, was not even close to being completed from the perspective of the two organization's cultures. As a result, there were some cultural clashes within the organization when I arrived.

Due to the growth the cooperative was experiencing, changes needed to be made within the organization quickly because the extensive growth was putting stress on the organization. This was my first CEO position and I was not skilled at managing change at this stage in my leadership journey. I'm sad to say I was more inclined to lean towards an authoritarian style of leadership where I would issue orders and expect people to follow them. This approach created some heartburn and this information was conveyed to the board of directors.

When this feedback was shared with me, my first response was built around ego. I felt threatened by the channel of communication between board members and employees. I had an open-door policy, but at this stage in my career that wasn't working. Looking back, it's obvious why; if people see that as an open door to a lion's den rather than to a safe and comfortable place where they can have an honest conversation and know they have been heard, they won't be inclined to knock on the door, much less walk through it.

Leadership lessons...

My first lesson from this experience is that taking an authoritative approach with people would have been more effective and appropriate, because I would have been more responsive and communicative. I would have expressed empathy and understanding in my conversations and set boundaries and expectations at a high level. An authoritative approach is one that has empathy and warmth, as well as clearly defined goals and expectations. In contrast is an authoritarian approach, which is when a leader uses their power to drive things. Sometimes we see an authoritarian style manifest as the "it is my way or the highway" approach.

Working through this situation took a lot of growth on my part and some very adept coaching from a very skilled board president to help me understand; that we would all do much better at handling those conversations if we saw what came out of them as information that we wouldn't otherwise have, and collectively decided how to act on this information.

We created an approach that allowed employees to talk directly to board members, with the understanding that this information would be reported to me and that I could decide how best to act on it. In doing this, we framed it as an exchange of information and were able to stay in alignment with the chain of command when it came to actually changing the organization or moving it forward.

This was a really important step that showed how I could continue as the manifestation of the board's decision. This meant I could show the board, the membership, and the employees that the board's decision to bring me on as CEO was a good one.

Ego: The idea of dialogue between board members and employees is one that it's important to pay close attention to. Remember that even though you may feel threatened by that dialogue, by approaching it with an open mind and seeing it as an opportunity for growth and overall improvement, you can turn this into a significant asset for the board, yourself as the manager, your employees, and your membership.

The nature of CEO-board relationships

The issues I've just discussed relating to communication might be less likely to occur if you are promoted to the position of CEO from within the cooperative you already work. If this is how you become CEO, chances are that you already have a good relationship with the various board members and this can certainly make your transition to this position go more smoothly.

However, even if you are promoted from within your organization, rather than joining as CEO from elsewhere, it's important to recognize that things are going to change for you as soon as you step into that CEO role. You are no longer a peer within your established peer group. You will not be a peer with your co-workers, and you won't be a peer with your board members. This is where the saying comes from that "it is lonely at the top". You will have close relationships, but they will be different, and that is okay. It is important to be at ease with yourself and the people you lead and, yes, you are also leading the board to a certain extent. Being at ease does not mean being any less respectful to the person or the position or role they have. Just as you will earn a new type of respect from your past peers, you must also keep a special level of respect for board members, no matter how "at ease" you feel. Stay humble, check your ego, be self-aware.

The unique relationship between the board and the CEO

As I mentioned earlier, when you become CEO it's important to remember that you are the physical embodiment of the board's decision and with that comes awesome responsibilities and amazing opportunities. It also leads to a unique relationship within an organization. I have seen CEOs who are visibly struggling in their roles and I've observed their frustration with the board and seen the board's frustration with their CEO. I can also say that I have experienced some similar stress as CEO.

It's important to remember that, while unique in many ways, the CEO-board relationship is like any other relationship you have in life, whether personal or professional, in that there will always be some type of conflict. It is simply the nature of being human that we don't always agree and see things from the same perspective. We have to learn to be comfortable in conflict and accept that it is a part of leadership and growth. You will learn that conflict and the related anxiety won't kill you, and if you look at it constructively, it will make you stronger and a better leader.

What we have to remember about the CEO-board relationship is that when decisions are made in the boardroom, they are made by the entire board. While all boards have their own cultures and operate differently, I believe one of the most important skills a board can have is the ability to unite behind a decision. Even though everyone on the board may not have voted for a particular decision, once that decision is made it's the responsibility of all the board members to enforce and support that decision.

Similarly, as the CEO, you have to support the board's decision, even if it's not the one you were hoping to receive. Any time that the board makes a decision that the CEO is unable or unwilling to support, it begins to erode the function and quality of the board-CEO relationship. Again, ego can play a part here, especially when the decision that has been made isn't yours. As a CEO, you have to get behind the board's decision and carry it forward as if it were yours.

There are bound to be times when there's a gap between your perspective as the CEO and that of the board. However, one of the things I've learned over the years is that boards process, consume and act on the information that the CEO and staff provide to them. If the information the board receives is good quality, the outcomes will likely be better; and if the information they receive is poor quality, the outcomes will reflect that poor quality.

Mike's leadership lesson: Trusting the magic of board decision making

Over the years, there have been a handful of instances where the board's ultimate decision was not one of, or even close to, my recommendations. This will happen to every CEO at some point, and how it's handled will truly define your career. I have seen CEOs use this opportunity to talk with their staff about how badly the board got this one wrong, and I have never seen that scenario work out for the good of the organization or its membership. I believe in the magic of the board decision-making process and the power of the diverse minds, experiences, and intuitions coming together to solve a problem.

When my board turned right, instead of the left I was looking for, more often than not they were right. There have been a few times where I struggled with the right turn they took, and in those situations I was able to see that I had failed in giving the board enough good information for them to reach the best decision. In these cases I assumed responsibility for making a mistake and told the board that I had made a mistake in not communicating and educating them thoroughly on the issue at hand. After assuming personal responsibility, I sought permission to reframe the matter. They always listened, many times they took the turn to the left that I had recommended. We always learned something when this happened and our mutual respect grew.

Leadership lessons...

When you make a recommendation to your board and they go in a different direction, your first reaction will likely be something along the lines of, "I can't believe they did that!" – especially when your ego kicks in. If you sit with that reaction and dwell on it, then it creates conflict and that doesn't serve anyone.

In my experience, boards generally get decisions right, you just don't know it at the time. You have to trust in the magic of the boardroom and the diversity and experience of your board members. However, if you reflect on the decision the board has made and assume that the magic worked, but you still can't get the decision to sit right, then chances are that you did not provide them with all the information you have on that topic.

At this point, you have to carefully consider everything you know about a topic and what wasn't conveyed to the board. When you have figured this out, you can go back to your board, tell them you made a mistake and share this additional information with them. When you reframe a decision in this way, oftentimes you'll see a change.

Self-awareness: You have to recognize when you have not shared all the relevant information with your board, and you need to be humble enough to admit your mistake. Rather than letting your ego kick in, think about what you could have done better.

Consider good information in terms of junk food versus healthy food. If you're responsible for providing nourishment to somebody, but all you're giving them is junk food, chances are they won't be as healthy as they would be in all aspects of their life if you were providing them with very healthy food. Information is food for the board; so, if the CEO wants the board to be strategically focused they need to give the board strategic information that connects the dots on the complex matters at hand.

If, however, the CEO wants the board to have a strategic focus but spends all their time talking about operational issues then over time that will grow into a larger and larger disconnect. Therefore, it's incumbent upon the CEO and the board's president to understand and agree where they are going to take the board and how the board is going to participate in the various functions of the cooperative.

Through my experience, I've found that if you want your board to think strategically you have to present information to them from a strategic perspective. If you do otherwise and spend all your time talking to your board about operational matters and then ask them to think strategically, you will run into conflict.

CEOs can often think of strategy as their domain – early in my career I certainly thought this way. I would develop these wonderful strategies about how we could do things and present these strategies to the board of directors. They would bless these strategies, largely because of trust, and I would leave the boardroom with this wonderful strategy and expect the organization to jump to it and begin executing it.

As I explained in Chapter 9, I learned very quickly that this was not going to be effective because while we could all point to a great strategy, its actual execution was not as strong. I realized that I needed to step off my "mountain" and not only involve the board of directors in its creation, but also the employees. This certainly takes a lot of time, but by involving the board, senior management and a select group of your high-potential and very capable subject-matter expert employees, you are able to understand the landscape around you, see more clearly what's happening in your environment, and then figure out potential ways to reframe threats and turn those into opportunities. From there you can take opportunities and turn them into definite, actionable items.

Doing this collectively and collaboratively at all levels in the organization and growing that into your finished project or product is a fantastic way to involve both the board and your team in your strategy. This means that the strategy you come up with is not the CEO's strategy rendered from a mountaintop, but the company's strategy, and everybody feels that they own a piece of it. In actual fact, everybody does actually own a piece of it because they have all contributed to its creation.

Different levels of trust

Building trust is an important part of the board-CEO relationship, but it's important to recognize that trust can be developed in many different ways. You have blind trust, for example, and in certain situations such as a crisis where you need to make rapid and immediate decisions, blind trust comes in really handy. Use blind trust very sparingly.

Then there's trust based on experience, where you've seen someone get decisions right so you trust them to make the right decisions in the future. To develop this kind of trust, you need to have a history of making good decisions.

However, if you want to build a level of trust that goes even deeper than this and that really gets to the heart of the culture – who we are, why we do what we do and how we're going to get to where we need to be – you have to involve people foundationally in the process.

The way to develop this kind of trust is by building an underlying commonality of your goals, how you look at the world and how you approach work. This is probably the richest and deepest form of trust you can develop between the board and the CEO, and even between the employees across the whole organization.

When you have this level of trust, everyone understands what's behind the curtain from a fundamental perspective. They might not agree with everything all of the time. But, if they know what's behind the curtain and why things are getting done, then it establishes a foundation and culture of trust that is far superior to the rate of right decisions versus wrong decisions that you make and even to blind trust that is occasionally needed in certain situations.

Maintaining trust in challenging times

One of the most important and powerful aspects of the board-CEO relationship is what happens when things go wrong, because (unfortunately) things will not always go right. When things are going well, the board-CEO relationship is very easy; it's when things go wrong that the strength of that relationship is truly tested.

As the CEO, there are innumerable opportunities for things to go wrong in your organization. I believe that it's not only the board-CEO relationship that is important in this scenario, but also the relationship between the CEO and the wider team. The CEO has to assume responsibility for everything that happens in the organization, good and bad. It's especially important that the CEO steps up when things go wrong and that they take responsibility for what went wrong, rather than throwing someone else under the bus. You can't point fingers or lay blame. Instead, you have to recognize the problem, accept responsibility for what happened, and show the board that you have a plan to correct the situation and ensure that whatever has gone wrong will never happen again.

I'm not going to pretend this is easy. In fact, it's very difficult to stand before a group of people, explain what happened, take personal responsibility, apologize and then go away and make it right.

Mike's leadership lesson: Operator, we have a problem

"Mike, we've had a cybersecurity breach, it's our telephone system..."

"What's happened?"

"Someone has hijacked the system and gained internal access to our telephone switch. They've harnessed our network of outgoing lines and we think they're making toll calls..."

"How long have they had access?"

"We're not sure, but we're working on shutting the whole system down."

The hackers had access to our phone system at PRECorp for 24 hours during this incident, during which time they made calls to an offshore number and ran up fraudulent toll charges in excess of seven figures. Fortunately, no member data was involved in this breach and I'm happy to say that we were able to come to a successful resolution of those charges with our provider.

However, as the CEO, it was my job to report this breach to the board and to explain what had happened. This breach of our phone system was caused by a failure to implement some fairly simple safeguards and it would have been very easy for me to stand in front of the board and lay that blame on somebody else, anyone else.

Instead, I stood in the breach and accepted responsibility for that seven-figure charge. I told the board that I was aware of our phone system and had knowledge of these capabilities within the system and acknowledged that it would have been an easy question to ask to check if we were implementing the necessary safeguards. In assuming responsibility for this, I shifted the conversation from being about who we were going to blame and the consequences of their mistake to how we would fix things and ensure this never happened again.

The outcome was that the board and staff sat down together to discuss this particular issue, as well as cyber security in general. Ultimately, this conversation resulted in our board having an increased sensitivity and heightened awareness of risk vulnerability in relation to our IT and cyber assets. Using this knowledge and by working together, we were able to come up with not only a strategy for our phone system, but also an overall cyber security strategy that was many years ahead of its time. We did this by creating a position within the organization to manage cyber security and we developed a company program to educate everyone about cyber security, monitor potential risks and to implement corrective action.

All things considered, this story ended well. We learned a valuable lesson and we were able to use this situation to launch a best-in-class cyber security program at PRECorp. This program has been in place for many years now and we have reached a level of maturity that is far ahead of other organizations of a similar size, in the cooperative world, in relation to how we manage our cyber security.

Leadership lessons...

If I had gone to the lowest common denominator and laid the blame for this incident on somebody else, I would have turned the conversation with my board into one focused on blame and consequence. By accepting responsibility myself, and promising the board that we wouldn't let this happen again, we were able to move the conversation on and have much more constructive outcomes.

In addition, everybody under me who perhaps shared responsibility for that particular breach became even more motivated to support what we were doing and prevent something similar from happening again. What could have been an ugly mess in the organization turned into a unifying cry that was ultimately supported by the board of directors with the resources we needed to help establish a best-in-class cyber security program.

The ability to stand up and take responsibility is certainly made easier when you have a high-trust relationship with your board. The way I think of it is that, as a CEO, you put relationship capital in the bank with the board by being reliable, trustworthy, open and transparent, and not shying away from having difficult conversations. All of these things add capital to your relationship bank and this gives you the confidence to be able to stand in the breach and do the right thing for the organization and its membership whenever a big event like this occurs.

Self-awareness: By being aware not only of yourself, but also of your relationship with your board and your team, you will find it easier to follow the right course of action and take responsibility when this is needed. To do this with confidence, you need to put capital in your relationship bank with your board.

Keeping it fresh

When I first came to PRECorp I thought I would be there for five to seven years. One of my most influential mentors, Doug Bursey, had told me that managers that stay too long get complacent and eventually the organization ends up serving them, instead of them serving the organization. I understood what Doug was saying and I also wondered how I would be able to "keep the pace" much beyond that seven-year timeframe. At the end of the first seven years, we had harvested much of the low-hanging fruit and the challenges and opportunities before us would require some very deep digging into the fabric and culture of the organization in order to be addressed.

I had survived the first seven years with tenacity, relentless energy and too much of an authoritarian leadership style. I think Doug's advice about moving on after five to seven years was grounded on the experience that, by seven years the manager had done all the things they were good at, they had leveraged their strengths, made a difference, and now it was time for another skill set to come in and do the same.

I spoke with my board about this and also expressed a desire to rein-vent myself and to consider letting go of those things that had helped me be successful so far. I explained that I thought these very things were also what was holding me back from serving the organization and its membership at an even higher level, and these could be things that might limit our future success. I asked the board to support my pursuit of an MBA and they agreed. This MBA was unique in that it focused on servant leadership development as much as business principles and strategy. I committed to another five years at PRECorp in order to have the company invest in supporting me in this program.

It might have been easier to follow Doug's plan, but the board had faith in me and the collective wisdom of the board realized that by focusing on servant leadership, we could effectively dive in on the toughest issues we were struggling with. I look back today after a 21-year career at PRECorp, and the MBA was the first of many re-inventions of myself. It showed me how I could be a more effective leader. Each of these steps was supported and encouraged through ongoing dialogue and feedback with the board. The board embraced the idea of annual CEO 360 evaluations as well as annual Employee Opinion Surveys, and the results and trends of this helped us keep it fresh. We don't shy away from feedback and self reflection and we have built on mutual respect while maintaining a sense of ease.

Working with your board is a key part of your job and your opportunity for growth. My suggestions are to be open, transparent and honest. Make feedback a welcome addition to all your conversations. Establish and respect boundaries, the varying roles of the players and the awesome magic of the boardroom process. Give your board good information and help them focus on what matters most.

Never forget that you are the embodiment of their most important decision.

CONCLUSION

Perhaps when you picked up this book you were curious about leadership and were hoping for a few takeaways for how you might up your game and improve your leadership skills. While I think this book has good takeaways no matter where you might be in your leadership journey, there is much more here than takeaways. This book invites you to see transformational leadership as a process not only for you, but also for the people and organization you serve. The invitation to dig deep is ever present throughout this book and hopefully it will inspire you in your journey to become a Leader Worth Following.

The concepts are easy to understand, yet a bit elusive to implement. The model involving the concept of leading yourself, leading teams, and leading organizations is not a new idea, but approaching that with a focus on self-awareness and empathy using the No-Os of leadership as guideposts is. There are many great leaders out there, and great leadership stories to go along with them. The best leaders, those who truly desire to serve, understand the power of knowing themselves first and then leading from a heart of service to others.

Giving instead of taking, serving instead of being served, and enriching others; these are the hallmarks of a Leader Worth Following. These are the results of paying attention to the No-Os of leadership. Hold your decisions, behaviors, and how you lead, against the backdrop of ego, libido, and dinero and you will be part of the transformational movement inspired by the No-Os of leadership.

Dig deep my friend, and the gold will find you.

If the concepts you have read about in this book have resonated on your leadership journey, please reach out to learn how I can help you further via https://noosofleadership.com/. I offer executive coaching opportunities based on my experiences both in business and the world. Through working on a Masters Degree in Clinical Mental Health Counseling, I am ideally positioned to offer both life and executive coaching, as well as to help you identify other areas of your life where you may be facing long-term issues and to make referrals to other professionals who can support you.

The reason this is so important, from a leadership development perspective, is that you cannot separate your work self from your personal self, so you want to make each as strong as they can possibly be. This book, along with my fictional book *The Antics,* form a practice that offers life coaching in addition to executive coaching opportunities to help people in every area of their lives. Our work selves and our personal selves are not two distinct pieces; they have to work together and be integrated to allow us to lead more fulfilling lives.

ABOUT THE AUTHOR

Mike is the CEO of Powder River Energy Corporation (PRECorp), a role he has held since 2000. Prior to joining PRECorp, Mike had worked for various other electric cooperatives in the USA. He holds an MBA from the Ken Blanchard School of Business and Grand Canyon University in Phoenix, Arizona and a BS degree in Electrical Engineering.

Mike has been coaching and developing executives for over two decades while, at the same time, continuing his own personal growth journey. This journey led him to author *The Antics,* a book about the fictional characters of Carence and Narcy who are locked in a dysfunctional relationship, and how Carence leaves the relationship behind and goes on his own healing journey. You can learn more about *The Antics* at www.theanticsbook.com

Mike is currently working on a Masters Degree in Clinical Mental Health Counseling at Grand Canyon University and hopes to augment his helping skills by becoming a licensed professional counselor and certified life coach.

He wants to use his experience and learnings to help develop the leaders of the future, and to support others on their leadership journeys. Mike is also dedicated to supporting his local community in Wyoming. In 2016, he was appointed to the Wyoming Business Council (WBC) board of directors. The WBC works with private businesses, state agencies, local governments, local economic development groups, partners and nonprofits to grow and diversify Wyoming's economy, create jobs and enhance the quality of life for everyone.

Prior to Mike's appointment at the WBC, he served Governor Dave Freudenthal and Governor Matt Mead as Chairman of the Wyoming Infrastructure Authority, a state entity focused on diversifying Wyoming's energy economy.

Made in the USA
Middletown, DE
05 July 2022

68502621R00119